Girolamo Savonarola

'Do you have faith? Yes: this is a great grace of God, for faith comes of his gift, not of your works, that no one may glory in them.'

Prison Meditations, *Girolamo Savonarola*

'Although some theological mud still adhered to the feet of that holy man, [Savonarola] nevertheless maintained justification by faith alone without works, and he was burned by the Pope.'

Martin Luther

Girolamo Savonarola

Douglas Bond
and Douglas McComas

 BOOKS

EP BOOKS
Faverdale North
Darlington
DL3 0PH, England

www.epbooks.org
sales@epbooks.org

EP BOOKS are distributed in the USA by:
JPL Fulfillment
3741 Linden Avenue Southeast,
Grand Rapids, MI 49548.

E-mail: sales@jplfulfillment.com
Tel: 877.683.6935

First published 2014

British Library Cataloguing in Publication Data available
ISBN: 978-17839-700-18

To our wives

Contents

Timeline

1495	Republic re-established in Florence
1497	Bonfire of the Vanities
1498	Ordeal by fire and arrest (March)
1498	Imprisonment and torture (April)
1498	Hanged and burned (May)

1

Man on fire

'*Siamo perduti!*' The cry echoed off the marble statues and fine stonework of the streets and plazas of Florence, Italy. 'We are ruined!' What Florentines feared had come upon them. It was 21 September 1494, and the birthplace of the Renaissance was paralyzed with dread. Greedy for blood, the army of the king of France had crossed the Alps and was on the march to Florence. In a matter of days Charles VIII's soldiers would be thundering at the gates of the city.

'The expedition of Charles VIII into Italy', wrote Edward Gibbon, 'changed the face of Europe.' In those gut-wrenching days, Florentine mothers and children cared little for what happened to the face of Europe; but they were horrified for their own lives. In despair, they crowded into the cathedral church of Santa Maria del Fiore, long-awaited innovation of the architectural genius, Filippo Brunelleschi (1377–1446). The Duomo had become the virtual symbol of the Renaissance. Since its completion in 1436, the cathedral's dome remains the largest masonry dome in the world, the grand marvel not only of the city, but of the entire cultural movement. One awed contemporary said the Duomo was 'vast enough to cover the entire Tuscan population with its shadow'.

With lecherous French soldiers slavering at her gates, terrified Florentines sought refuge under that vast dome. They had gathered to hear the prior of San Marco, the fiery preacher who had expelled the Medicis and their tyrannies. That man was Girolamo Savonarola (1452–1498).

When Savonarola ascended the high pulpit, his congregation — numb with fear — longed for some words of comfort from his lips. He looked out on their upturned faces. 'For behold, I will bring a flood of waters upon the earth,' the Dominican friar gave out his text, 'to destroy all flesh' (Genesis 6:17). The sombre manner in which he read the sacred words sent a shudder through every man, woman and child that stood before him. Eyewitness to the sermon, philosopher Pico della Mirandola said that Savonarola's terrifying words made his hair stand on end. And with the preacher's every word, the French army came on to their destruction — just as he had prophesied.

Savonarola's world

Savonarola's world reads like the guest list at a royal banquet, a veritable 'who's who' of celebrities. He breathed the air of the famous and the infamous, the notable and the notorious, the gifted and the great.

Born in Ferrara in 1452, he shared a birth year with Renaissance artist Leonardo da Vinci. As Savonarola's mother laboured to deliver her son, Ghiberti was completing the bronze doors of the Florentine baptistery, dubbed the 'Gates of Paradise' by Michelangelo.

When Savonarola was taking his first halting steps, Johann Gutenberg was casting the final type for his printing press in Mainz, and when he was in his terrible twos, first editions of the Gutenberg Bible were available for purchase. Then, when peach fuzz was showing on Savonarola's upper lip, the 'Prince of Humanists', Erasmus of Rotterdam, was born. Banking tycoon Lorenzo de Medici began his lavish rule of Florence when Savonarola would have been old enough to get his driver's licence. Significantly, 1469 also marked the birth of the Florentine codifier of pragmatic politics, Niccolo Machiavelli (1469–1527).

A medical student at Bologna when Copernicus was born in 1473, Savonarola was twenty-five when Caxton printed Chaucer's *Canterbury Tales* in England; author of *Utopia*, Sir Thomas More, was born a year later. While Savonarola delivered his first halting sermons in Florence, Botticelli was painting frescoes in Rome. In 1483, when Savonarola was thirty-one, Martin Luther was born in Eisleben. Preaching through Genesis in Florence in 1492, Savonarola may have heard of Columbus's first voyage of discovery to the New World, though the death of Lorenzo de Medici and the transfer of power to his son may have kept him from giving the event much thought.

Two years later, according to Savonarola's prophecy, Charles VIII of France invaded Italy, with Pope Alexander VI fleeing for his life. In Savonarola's final years in Florence, da Vinci was busy painting his masterpiece, *The Last Supper*. And while Savonarola wrote his *Prison Meditations* in the tower of Palazzo Vecchio, Michelangelo was chiselling the final details on his *Pieta* in Rome.

Preaching the Scriptures

Savonarola was first and last a preacher, an impassioned orator with a message burning within him that could not be silenced. With force and clarity, he delivered his sermons to vast audiences pressing their way into the Duomo, as many as 12,000 people at a time. Attempting to copy down what Savonarola was preaching, one listener confessed, 'I was overcome by weeping and could not go on.'

In a day when virtually no one preached the Scriptures, Savonarola was an unabashed preacher of the Bible. For this alone he deserves the esteem of all Christians. Describing other preachers in Renaissance Florence, he said, 'They speak against pride and ambition, but they are immersed in it up to the eyes. They preach chastity, but they keep concubines. They recommend fasting, but they live luxuriously.' What is more, these false preachers delivered their false sermons in a language most of their listeners did not understand. Savonarola would have none of that.

An important priority of the Renaissance was the return to the vernacular, the language of the people. Scholars sought out ancient manuscripts from the classical world: Virgil, Cicero, Aristotle — anything Greek and Roman. In the century before Savonarola, Petrarch (1304–1374), 'Father of Renaissance Humanism', not only gathered manuscripts from antiquity, but he began composing love sonnets in the vernacular.

Savonarola had other interests in the vernacular. Jerome's fourth-century Latin Bible had been in the 'vulgar' or common language the average person understood. But the medieval church had distorted the Latin Bible into an upper-storey sacred language and made it a high crime to translate its holy words into the tongue of the peasantry. Wed this with the Catholic doctrine declaring the pope to be sole interpreter of the Bible's meaning, and you have the perfect storm for theological tyranny.

Unique in his day, Savonarola delivered his sermons, not in Latin, but in the Florentine Italian the people in Tuscany understood. His was primarily expository preaching through books of the Bible as Luther, Calvin and the Reformers would do a generation later. His message was more like that of the Hebrew prophets: a declaration of the holiness of God, a decrying of rebellion against God's will and ways, the promise of judgement at the hands of an angry God, concluding with an earnest appeal to repentance.

Sin city

And Florentines had plenty for which to repent! Bankrolled by Medici wealth, Florence rivalled Sodom and Gomorrah.

Along with gambling and partying, prostitution had become the ordinary activity of the city, the *via dei Pellicciai* notorious for its taverns and brothels. When the west entrance to the Duomo became so crowded with prostitutes parading themselves like street venders, even loose-living officials called for restriction of the trade in the cathedral precinct.

Savonarola missed no one in his denouncements against wickedness. 'I am like unto the hail,' he said, 'which pelts everyone who is out in the open air,' including the carnal-living clergy that choked the streets of Florence. Popes and prelates, painters and princes — all fell under the hailstorm of his impassioned preaching.

'The divine word from the lips of Savonarola,' one historian described his preaching, 'descended not amongst his audience like the dews of heaven. It was the piercing hail, the sweeping whirlwind, the destroying sword.' And thousands swarmed the nave of the cathedral to hear him preach. Historian William Robinson Clark wrote: 'The cathedral was crowded with eager listeners. Savonarola was becoming more and more the mind, the conscience, the will of Florence.'

Preaching and art

Ask a dozen people who Savonarola was and you are likely to get a dozen people who will tell you that he was an art-hating Philistine determined to make sure no one in Florence had any more fun. This is a convenient spin to debunk Savonarola so we can get back to the really important business of gushing about what da Vinci or Michelangelo could do with paint or marble — which was nothing short of astonishing.

Impressive as Renaissance art is, art becomes idolatry when the created thing usurps the Creator, when the temporal trumps the eternal. Savonarola knew that Florence was doomed if rebellion against God's law continued unchecked. He loved Florence, especially her most vulnerable citizens: women and children and the dependent poor. He also knew that blatant immorality produced societal dysfunction that harmed the weakest, and enslaved and impoverished people.

Hence, Savonarola was determined to do what he could to halt the moral freefall in Florence. For him, art and culture must not be used as excuses to ignore the eternal condemnation that awaited Florence for her sins. Remain on the path of decadence and Savonarola knew that temporal poverty awaited the city in this life, and hell and damnation in the next. 'O Lord! Arise,' he prayed, 'and come to deliver thy Church from the hands of devils, from the hands of tyrants, from the hands of iniquitous prelates.' Savonarola believed that the primary means by which God would bring about such deliverance was biblical preaching.

Unlike his contemporaries, Savonarola practised what he preached. It was not the Medicis, the painters, or the priests who shouldered the responsibility to clean up the societal messes they had helped create with their moral decadence. It was Savonarola who implemented plans to care for the neglected and abandoned wives and children, the dependent poor, and the sick and needy.

Misguided as they may seem to moderns, Savonarola's 'Bonfires of the Vanities', into which he encouraged people to hurl their pornographic pictures, their gambling devices, and their facepaint, were designed to break the chains enslaving the city and its culture. Even the acclaimed Botticelli — famous for his nude painting affectionately called 'Venus on the Half-Shell' by art enthusiasts — fell under conviction and cast some of his paintings of pagan themes onto the conflagrations.

In all of this, Savonarola was more a reformer of morals than of doctrine, more in the role of a forerunner, a John the Baptist, than of an apostle Paul. His role was to decry wickedness and to call men to repentance, thereby to prepare the way for the theological clarity of his successors in the Reformation.

Preaching love

Yet the question remains: Why include a Roman Catholic in a series of biographies on Reformational heroes? After all, Savonarola's motto, as translated by some, 'A man knows as much as he works,' sounds suspiciously like works-righteousness. If so, why feature him with those who stood their ground precisely against works-righteousness, who risked all to proclaim the biblical doctrine of justification by faith alone — *not* by works?

In his classic biography on Savonarola, the celebrated Italian historian and statesman Pasquale Villari translates Savonarola's motto with a different sense: 'As much as one knows, so much one does,' which sounds at least somewhat more like the apostle Paul who longed to know more of the love of Christ, so that transformed by divine love, he might overflow with gospel love for others.

Villari agrees that Savonarola's doctrine at first blush sounds like the doctrine of works, but he immediately continues: 'were it not rather the doctrine of love'. He draws this conclusion from Savonarola's description of saving love: 'This love is likewise a gift of the Lord; it is a fire that kindleth all dry things, and whoever is disposed unto it shall forthwith find it descend into his heart and set it aflame.'

When a man calls salvation 'a gift of the Lord', he cannot be quite so far away from the justification by faith alone preached by Reformers in the next generation. To be sure, Savonarola had a great deal to say about law and good works. But he was clear that 'Nothing can be done save by the impulse of love. Love easily and sweetly fulfilleth the whole law of God.'

And where did this love come from? Savonarola's preaching was full to the brim with the source: the love of Jesus.

> Love bound Him to the pillar, love led Him to the cross, love raised Him from the dead and made Him ascend into heaven, and thus accomplishing all the mysteries of our redemption. This is the true and only doctrine, but in these days the preachers teach nothing but empty subtleties.

When a Dominican friar uses the terminology of Christ 'accomplishing all the mysteries of our redemption', he sounds like he has been reading the Reformers. In a sense he had been. In his youth Savonarola discovered and read Augustine, the Early Church Father of choice for the Reformers. There is little doubt that he would have read this or material like it from Augustine's writings:

> ... those who are delivered from punishment by grace are called, not vessels of their own virtues, but 'vessels of mercy' (Rom.9:23). Whose mercy? God's, the One Who sent Christ Jesus into the world to save the sinners whom He foreknew, and predestined, and called, and justified, and glorified. Now, who could be so madly insane as to fail to give inexpressible thanks to the mercy which liberates whom it chooses?

Under such an influence, as Savonarola matured, he began in his own writings to sound much more like he believed this from Augustine than the enslaving works-righteousness of medieval Roman Catholicism.

Vanguard Reformer

Savonarola, however, had little access to the more developed theological minds to the north. John Wycliffe had his Bradwardine, and John Huss had his John Wycliffe. All the Reformers began on the road to Reformation by decrying corruption within the Church of Rome; only later did they come to see that the root problem was a theological one. Alas, Savonarola's life was cut short before he came to an unequivocal expression of the doctrines of grace and the pure gospel of Christ alone.

We may further infer the theological direction in which Savonarola was travelling by the twin facts that on 13 May 1497 he was excommunicated by the pope, and that his published writings were placed on the Index of Prohibited Books by the Council of Trent and thrown on the fire by the Inquisition. Clearly Roman Catholics felt that his writings, his doctrine, his legacy — the man himself — deserved a place on their bonfires of heresies.

At the end of the day, Savonarola's partially formed theology should not surprise us; he was a theological vanguard, and vanguards rarely are the final codifiers of theology. What is clear, however, is that Savonarola was on a trajectory away from the theological synergism of the Roman Church. And in the next generation, Luther and the theologians of the Reformation would plant in the fertile ground harrowed by the zealous preaching of Savonarola.

Publishing vanguard

Yet another distinctive of Savonarola's ministry secures for him a lasting place in church history. No single man captured so early and so completely the power of moveable type printing as did Savonarola. From 1492 to his death in 1498, no sooner had he preached a sermon or set words to parchment than his supporters had it off to the printer.

Printers proliferated in Renaissance Florence, and all of them published Savonarola's works, but especially Bartolomeo de'Libri, who printed nearly half of all editions of his works.

In the final years of his preaching and leadership in Florence, Savonarola became without rival the most widely published author of the fifteenth century. In the last four years of his ministry, 100 separate editions of his sermons were published in Florence alone. Meanwhile, editions of his work were being published in France and in Germany. Illustrators eagerly sharpened their chisels to create woodcuts for Savonarola's printed sermons.

In the next generation it was Martin Luther who took up Savonarola's publishing mantle. Luther so valued him as a harbinger of the Reformation that he published an edition of Savonarola's *Prison Meditations*, offering glowing praise for the Florentine preacher in the preface.

Heart aflame

A voice crying in a moral wasteland, Savonarola was consumed with zeal for God's glory in Renaissance Florence. His storied life was replete with more danger and loneliness, intrigue and treachery, than he would face from the French army that September day in 1494. Yet was Savonarola steadfast in a world of moral decadence, single-minded in a day of spiritual decay — not unlike our own day.

Still more, Savonarola was consumed with a gift: the love of Christ, the fire that had ignited his own heart and set it aflame. That love, that fire, would cost him everything.

2

Early life

In the northern Italian city of Ferrara, young Girolamo Savonarola (1452–1498) would have daily walked under the massive towers of the fourteenth-century Castello Estense, one of Europe's most imposing fortresses. Encircled by an impassable moat, it was built by Nicollo II d'Estes to protect the ruling family from bloody peasant uprisings — the likeliest thing on the cards given their dictatorial brutalities.

Walking pensively along the cobbles before the castle, young Girolamo could not have foreseen that in 1536 the theologian of the Reformation, John Calvin, would preach within the walls of that same castle before Renee of Ferrara, zealous supporter of the Reformation. Nor could the boy have had any notion that God would make him a forerunner of that Reformation — and that it would cost him his life.

With the city's central district behind him, his wanderings would have taken him past the Romanesque Cathedral of San Giorgio, its magnificent architecture inspiring his early love of the Church. Lost in thought, he would have strolled the wide lanes and narrow alleyways lined with tall stone houses and shops topped with red-tile roofs. He would have breathed the aromas of baking bread and roasting garlic commingling with the stench of manure and human waste.

In this setting Savonarola's parents raised their seven children; their third child, Girolamo, was born 12 September 1452. While other boys his age played in the hot sun along the cool banks of the Po di Volano River, he preferred the company of a dim candle and books. In a world where plague and warfare were as normal to him as social networking and lattés are in ours, Savonarola as a youth made friends with the Bible, Augustine and Aquinas.

Early nurture

In 1440, Michele Savonarola, young Savonarola's grandfather, had been summoned from the northern Italian city of Padua to be the d'Este family physician in Ferrara. A great lover of books, Michele had served as a professor of medicine at Padua University. In one of the number of books he authored, he gives us a window into their world. He wrote of preventative measures he developed to fight plague: fumigation, keeping away from infected people, and covering the mouth while coughing and talking.

After a day of enduring the rot of court and the horror of his practice, Savonarola's grandfather took pleasure in his grandson's blossoming intellect and interest in the Scriptures. Being a medieval doctor was a brutal business. Medical procedures were performed with ineffective anaesthesia and often ended in grief for the patient's family. Understanding of sanitation and the causes of infection were still mysteries, so the sick were as apt to die from the treatment as from the disease. His grandfather's evident Christian sentiments had a profound effect on Savonarola, helping shape his spiritual appetite for God's Word. Savonarola's father carried on the role as family physician in court, though his mother was thought a bit too principled for the decadence and intrigue of the d'Este court.

Few other details of Savonarola's childhood survive — except the trail of tears left from his adolescent love for the girl who lived across the street. So smitten was he by her charms that he set down feverish love poetry to her with his pen, a fitting beginning for the man who would be the most widely published author in the fifteenth century. But it ended in heartbreak. Savonarola's family income was more than a few ducats too lean to make it an equitable match. And there was the matter of his nose. Termed aquiline by his supporters, his critics would have employed other verbiage for a nose rivalling the shape, if not the size, of a spring zucchini.

The Renaissance

Savonarola's world was undergoing radical changes. A generation before his birth, Cosimo de Medici's (1389– 1464) agents scoured Europe for ancient manuscripts to fill his library. The Godfather of Florence, Cosimo invested a fortune sponsoring the arts and appeasing the Dominicans by lavishly rebuilding the monastery of San Marco. To the north, the first family of Ferrara was in their two-hundredth year of overseeing the walled city. The d'Este family had similar enthusiasms and gave bags of florins to support the Ferrara school of art, which hosted artists Bellini and Titian.

A thousand miles to the east, recent events unwittingly fed the renewed hunger for the learning of antiquity. The Turkish sultan had finally breached the walls of Constantinople with cannons capable of lobbing ordnance the weight of a Volkswagen. As the fortifications crumbled and the Muslims butchered Christians in the church of Saint Sophia, Greek scholars fled west bringing remnants of their classical libraries with them. The final collapse of the Roman Empire of the east and the resulting surge of Greek and Latin writings from antiquity continued to fuel the rebirth of Italy.

Infatuated with anything not Christian, Renaissance humanists gave themselves to ancient manuscripts as if they were God-breathed. This eagerness to push divine revelation aside in favour of man-made authority championed by the Renaissance was, by no means, an anomaly. History confirms that in every age men eagerly 'exchange the truth about God for a lie' (Romans 1:25). Europe was rushing headlong into a rebirth of that lie, the very lie that Savonarola would be commissioned to unmask.

Schooling

Many a father has told his son, 'Be a lawyer or a doctor'; few have said, 'Be a friar'. Hans Luther would urge his son to be a lawyer; Niccolo Savonarola urged his son to follow the family tradition and be a doctor, and that meant the University of Bologna, Italy's metropolis of letters, and a Bologna degree would lay the foundation for success whatever he would become.

From all over Europe students came to learn civil and canon law. They brought with them their languages and culture, and turned Bologna into a voguish international community. In this environment Savonarola rolled up the sleeves of his tunic and commenced the study of literature, history and philosophy.

The centuries have effected little fundamental change on university towns. It may have been 500 years ago, but young men far from home made Herculean efforts to showcase their virility and independence. This not only bewildered Savonarola, but repelled him as well. On all sides young men strutted about in tights and outrageous party-coloured costumes, completing their image with bizarre hats. The fifteenth-century version of hipster had its female equivalent too; young women wore dresses with detachable sleeves and tight bodices that left little to the imagination. Young Savonarola grieved at the rampant immorality and blasphemy surrounding him. In a letter home, he wrote:

> To be considered a man here, you must defile your mouth with the most filthy, brutal, and tremendous blasphemies. If you study philosophy and food arts you are considered a dreamer; if you live chastely and modestly, a fool; if you are pious, a hypocrite; if you believe in God, an imbecile.

Conscious of his sin and impending damnation, he spent hours in prayer and fasting, confessing his evils and depriving himself of food for days at a time. On his first visit home from university, he had no cavalier tales of carousing and drinking; his parents looked aghast at a pale, gaunt, sober young man.

While his classmates ate, drank and were merry, Savonarola longed for peace with God. There was no justification by faith alone to be heard from the Semi-Pelagianism of the Roman Catholic Church surrounding him. He lived in a paroxysm of fear, daily terrified that he might have committed a mortal sin. So he deprived himself, hoping to find comfort for his soul by inflicting hardship on his body, his self-denial taking on more and more drastic measures. During the Lenten season of 1447 he found temporary relief for his troubled conscience in a church-sponsored 'bonfire of the vanities' wherein students were invited to burn worldly possessions as a means of winning the favour of God; it was one of his few good memories of college.

Meanwhile he continued writing poetry. He expressed the convictions that would propel him to his future role in a poem he entitled *The Ruin of the World*:

> Earth is so pulled down by every vice
> That it will never stand again.
> Avoid all those who put on purple,
> Flee from palaces and ostentatious loggias,
> Speaking to the few alone,
> For you will be the enemy of the world.

Between the lines, one hears the loneliness of an upright man who would eventually be the enemy of the world and at war with the Church that dominated that world.

Change

When Savonarola's grandfather died and the family income began dwindling, his mother and father directed their son to medical school. Dutifully, he followed their wishes, but within weeks he realized that he no longer belonged in the university. Desperate to escape the darkness and filth surrounding him, he sought spiritual peace by fleeing home. But through the thin, cramped walls of the family home in Ferrara, he heard sighs, tears and bitter words: how would they pay for food, and what about his sisters' dowries? If only Savonarola would become a doctor and support the family.

The conflict mounted over the following weeks. Savonarola withdrew to his room, unshaven and unbathed, staring at cracked walls and breathing stale air. His industrious mother bit her lip; she had little time for an idle son who contributed nothing to the family larder. One day he lay on his back strumming a lute, every pluck acting as a drop of fat on the fire of his mother's temper. 'Son,' she said when she'd had enough, 'this is a sign of parting.'

In 1475, the year Michelangelo was born, and the night of Ferrara's spring festival, twenty-three-year-old Savonarola knew he had to act. While his family watched the acrobats

and jugglers and gazed skyward at bursting fireworks,
Savonarola packed his things and left home for good.

Dominican friar

Savonarola knew where he belonged. He belonged in the
monastery. By the fifteenth century, all monasteries observed
variations of the sixth-century Rule of Saint Benedict, a rigid
code designed to mortify the flesh and earn the favour of
God. Savonarola set out for the Dominican monastery in
Bologna, the order established in 1215 by Saint Dominic.
Leaving behind his lute, Savonarola donned the dark, coarse
habit of a Blackfriar Dominican.

Here he dedicated his life to God through prayer, penance,
solitude and self-denial. Vowing chastity and poverty, he
commenced the monastic life, vainly attempting to achieve
by his efforts what only grace can accomplish. By fasting to
the point of starvation, self-flagellating to mortify the flesh,
and living in quarters that would have troubled a Spartan
hoplite (foot soldier), Savonarola heartily entered into the
life of a friar, thereby attempting to release his soul from
bondage to his body. And here, by the study of history,
theology, canon law, and the Church Fathers, he would
prepare for a life of preaching.

Once ensconced at the Dominican order in Bologna,
Savonarola wrote a letter to his parents, dated 25 April 1475.
In spite of the recent falling out, his words show respect
toward parents who had loved and nurtured him.

My honoured father, I doubt not at all that my departure hath been to you painful and distressing; and I know it to have been the more distressing from the fact that I left you secretly and unknown to you. Yet I would that by this letter my mind and intention may be fully revealed unto thee, that thus thou may be of a better courage and may understand that I was led unto the purpose in question by no means in that light and childish spirit as I hear is believed by many persons.

He knew the gossip surrounding his departure, and he knew that he somewhat deserved it. But he felt compelled to unburden his heart to his parents, to show them his real motive for taking such an irrevocable step:

The chief reason which led me to the religious life and to a monastery, namely, the boundless misery of this world and the extreme unrighteousness of most men, the adulteries, thefts, idolatries, impurities, and hideous blasphemies, unto which this age hath so far reached that there may be found none that doeth good. For which cause I would often repeat with tears, 'Haste thee, haste to escape from a land that is cruel and greedy.' Now hath God, in His own good time, of His exceeding love towards me, at length shown unto me a way into which, unworthy though I be, I have entered and on which I have held.

He further reasoned with his father, arguing in his own defence, even resolving to rather die than to turn from the monastic life he had entered.

Is it not a fitting and glorious work of virtue for a man to avoid the defilements of this world? For a man to live the life of reason and not, as do the beasts, the life of sense? Moreover, should I not rightly be held the most foolish and the most ungrateful of men thus vehemently to have prayed God that he would open unto me right ways and show unto me the path wherein I should walk if, when He deigned so to do, I were to turn away and wander from the path? O my Jesus, a thousand times rather may I die than ever be guilty in Thy sight of so deep an ingratitude!

He was neither the first nor the last child to appeal to his own death to show the depth of his commitment to his chosen path, but for Savonarola this was no manipulative pretext. He was in earnest. It is clear that he had discussed these things many times in the home, and he here resumes his appeals to his father:

Thou must not weep. Nay, thou must render unceasing thanks to the Lord Jesus in that he hath granted unto thee a son and those two-and-twenty years hath kept him safe and sound.

Finally, he begged his father to

... do your utmost to console and strengthen my mother, of whom and of thyself I do very earnestly beseech that ye would give me your parental blessing; I, on my part, will constantly pray unto the Lord for the salvation and entire well-being of your souls.

Savonarola may have felt that his words would convince his family of the righteousness of his path, but he was mistaken. They tearfully appealed to him to return to the family and his home. He replied but now in an augmented tone:

> *You are blind. Why do you still weep and lament? You hamper me, though you should rejoice. What can I say if you grieve yet, save that you are my sworn enemies and foes to virtue? If so, then I say to you, 'Get ye behind me, all ye who work evil.'*

Harsh as his words seem to our ears, Savonarola was in earnest, a man on fire for the glory of God in his life. His eyes fixed on the goal he believed God had set before him, his was to be a life lived with his back against the defilements of the world and against his family, a life of preparation for death.

At his own request, possibly to soothe his broken heart, Savonarola took on the worst of duties at the convent — cleaning the latrines. As he went about his duties, to counter the taunts of the devil, he memorized large portions of the Bible, a practice that would feed his mind and heart for the escalating taunts of the enemy in his future ministry.

3

Monastic life

Light-headed from fasting, his back bloodied from flagellation, Savonarola was forced to continue without family approval. His superiors attempted to keep him from destroying himself and urged him to pursue his learning. But he was suspicious of the humanism creeping into theological studies: 'I have not entered religion to exchange the Aristotle of the world for the Aristotle of the cloister.' Amongst the stone walls and cloisters of the monastery, he turned from Aristotle and began studying the Bible. Later he recalled these years as the happiest of his life. For the moment, living silently with bells, rosary beads and incense felt like a perfect escape.

But only for a time. He soon realized the monastery he thought would be a paradise was no different from the outside. Men entered the cloister for a variety of motives: some were doing penance for past sins, others to hide from their past, and some to avoid responsibility for present crimes. Priors and abbots were often politically motivated priests using the cloister for personal advancement. The warring factions of politics and the Church bewildered Savonarola. Still more he was disgusted by the blatant violation of vows. Men who had solemnly taken vows of celibacy and poverty stained those vows by consorting with mistresses and by collecting fine art and relics. It seemed that the moral character of the Church had eroded to dust.

In perplexity, he wrote a sequel to his poem *Ruin of the World* entitled *Ruin of the Church*, wherein he personified the Church and carries on a conversation with her. 'Where are the ancient candour, charity, and doctrine?' he asks. The Bride of Christ replies: 'When I beheld proud ambition penetrating Rome and contaminating all things, then I retired to this place where I spend my life in mourning.' Seeing the cuts and bruises on her body, Savonarola asks: 'Who has done this to you?' The Church replies: 'A false proud whore, the whore of Babylon.' He makes a request: 'Oh God, Lady, that I might be the one to rend those false wings?' She silences him with her words: 'It may not be. No tongue of man may chide nor battle in my behalf. Mark my request: Weep and be silent. This seems to be best.'

These literary exchanges make clear Savonarola's mounting criticism of the Church and the false clergy that sits in her halls of power, but also his reluctance to openly denounce the corruption. However, that would change with time.

One day, after the usual meal of bread, vegetables and wine, he stared at a painting of Saint Dominic holding his finger to his lips. Ironically, both silence and preaching were parts of the rule of the Dominican order. Dominican friar preachers were the Lord's hounds, the missionaries of the church. He buried his face in the sleeve of his cowl. Was this God calling him out of the cloister into the world as a preacher? 'What now, Lord?' he cried, peeking through his fingers. 'Is it to be missionary work abroad?' He knew that Iberian navigators had circumnavigated Africa, discovering heathen tribes in need of Christianity. Was God calling him to preach the message to the heathen in faraway lands? Or was it something else? He was in torment. There was bountiful work to be done bringing the heathen to the faith. 'Could it be preaching?'

His prior was aware that Savonarola's cowl was cut from the cloth of sincerity; he also knew that, despite his obvious deficiencies in the pulpit, the young friar from Ferrara had the temperament, genius and passion that make a good preacher. So he arranged for Savonarola to preach in a small church nearby the monastery. When the day came, Savonarola ascended the pulpit, eyeing the paintings of saints and demons lining the walls and seemingly watching him; they awed him; they terrified him; they mocked him.

What followed was painful. He stammered; he mumbled; he lost his place in his notes. When it finally ended, the listeners, accustomed to the polished oratory of a university town, shook their heads, and rolled their eyes in disdain as they exited the church.

Cringing, but determined, he sought advice from the experts. The masters of elocution stressed cadence, rhetorical devices and gestures, and seemed to care far more about style than content. Savonarola felt like they were training him to be an actor in a tragedy, not a preacher in a pulpit proclaiming the Word of God.

And then in 1481 he received word that he was being transferred to the priory in Ferrara. 'The brothers must be in great need of workers,' he murmured at the news. It was certainly no promotion, and being called to the priory in his hometown placed him on the doorstep of the family who had rejected his calling in life.

What could God have in store for him back in Ferrara? Watching the ferrymen row the boat on the Po River, every stroke bringing him closer to his home, he may have begun to muse on the ease and rhythm of the men's motion, and it may have renewed his resolve to press on in his desire to develop effective preaching skills. And then, as sailors will do, one of them broke into a string of blasphemies, in the hearing of other passengers, including women and children.

Savonarola felt the heat rising in his temples, and he clenched the gunwale until his fingers ached. Before he entirely realized what he was doing, he heard himself speaking. 'Men shall be lovers of their own selves, covetous, boasters, proud, blasphemers,' he was saying, and he was saying it loudly, with passion and conviction. 'For these things the wrath of God is coming.' The Scripture he had committed to memory in his earliest days in the monastery had instantly come to his lips. The sailors fumbled at their oars, staring opened-mouthed at the friar with the large nose and the fire in his eyes. He may have been as astonished as they were, but no more so than when the foulest among them fell to his knees, begging the friar to grant him forgiveness. He would remember the power of scriptural authority and true conviction for the rest of his days.

Enduring taunts and jabs from childhood playmates, perhaps even the hauteur of the girl he thought he had loved, tensions mounted between the northern Italian city-states that escalated to war. After a short time, he was mercifully reassigned farther south to the rolling hills of Tuscany.

San Marco

Savonarola's new assignment was the freshly refurbished San Marco convent within the ramparts of Florence, the centre of learning, art and culture. A favourite retreat of Cosimo de Medici, tourists today come to gaze in wonder at the walls and living quarters of San Marco, adorned with Fra Angelico's (1395–1455) inspiring paintings. Daily Savonarola walked to his work down the cobblestoned streets toward the massive cathedral of Santa Maria del Fiore, Brunelleschi's Duomo. In 1463 when the last brick had been fitted in the massive dome, Florence's prestige skyrocketed.

At the cathedral Savonarola turned west down the busy streets lined with shops, silk and satin merchants looking with disdain at the plain black habit of the friar. Several hundred yards farther and he would arrive at the dull brown façade of San Lorenzo's. Housing spectacular artwork within its walls, the Medici's parish church was no backwater pulpit. Sensing his potential, Savonarola's prior resolved to give him another opportunity. San Lorenzo's was to be, at least for a time, Savonarola's pulpit.

For his first sermon, like a fresh-faced seminarian, he was determined to keep to his script. Looking out on the faces of the congregants from the spectacular bronze pulpit crafted by the famous sculptor Donatello (1386–1466), he felt keenly his many shortcomings as an orator. Heavy on the Bible, his words fell on sophisticated listeners more accustomed to the man-centred rhetoric of the humanists. With each sermon, fewer people turned out to hear Savonarola preach. At last he looked out on a sparse congregation of but twenty-five faithful souls.

'Father,' a congregant told him after a particularly dull exposition, 'there is no denying your doctrine is true, useful, and necessary, but your manner in presenting it is lacking in grace, especially as we have the example of Fra Mariano before our eyes.'

Savonarola cringed. Fra Mariano epitomized the theatrics and eloquent delivery his trainers had urged him to assume. Mariano spoke with such intellectual elocution, it mattered little what he said. 'He was great in the pulpit to more than human proportions,' one hearer gushed. 'He speaks, and I am all ears.' Mariano was the erudite celebrity preacher of the day, and he gave the sophisticated Florentines just what they wanted.

But Savonarola knew what they needed. 'Florid speech and elegance must yield,' said Savonarola, 'to the simplicity of sound doctrine.' But Florentines had itching ears, and Savonarola was not scratching where they wanted. He was dismissed as a failure and reassigned to the training of novices.

Zealous young pastors, take heart from this stage in Savonarola's ministry. The man who would become the most powerful preacher of the fifteenth century just got 'drop-kicked' from yet another preaching assignment. Dejected and discouraged, little could he know that soon the tables would turn, and Mariano and every other preacher in Florence would look with envy on Savonarola.

Plodding

In Savonarola's despair, the enemy went on the offensive. His body and soul were the battleground, and the Prince of Darkness seemed to be winning the fight. Walking the grim streets, he grieved at the darkness and slavery all about him. Everywhere he turned there were people enslaved to prostitution, homosexuality and drunkenness. Maybe the devil had already won. But his greatest grief was that the Church and her shepherds were no better, plunging into the same cesspool of corruption as the secular society.

Savonarola would fall asleep at night praying that Satan's arrest and destruction would come immediately. But he was heart-sick each morning to awaken to the same filth and corruption; Christ had not returned in triumph and judgement. A new day brought only renewed spiritual warfare. 'I am still flesh like you,' he wrote to his father, 'and the senses are unruly to reason, so that I must struggle cruelly to keep the demon from leaping on my back.'

'Struggle cruelly' was no mere metaphor for Savonarola. Daily he unfurled his whip and flogged himself; the greater the struggle with sin, the more stripes he inflicted on himself. As the leather ripped his skin and blood ran down his back, he hoped to teach his body the pain that awaited it when it sinned. So determined was he to expunge sin from himself, his face became set in a permanent squint with his lips pursed white with resolution.

In 1486 his prior, weary of watching his apprentice take Semi-Pelagianism to its logical limits, sent him up the Po River valley to Lombardy. The prior hoped that time away from the frivolities of Florence would soothe Savonarola's conscience and give him peace.

The clean air of the Italian Alps and lush green of the foothills were a welcome change for Savonarola from the corruptions of Florence. The simple peasant folks welcomed him, and their plain dress and unsophisticated manner was refreshing to him. More importantly, they listened intently to Savonarola's preaching and received his message with open hearts. He spoke to them gently, like they were novices at San Marco. Two years of ministry in the Alps matured his preaching and shepherding. His superiors breathed a sigh of relief; Savonarola had found his place.

But it was not so. His torments had continued, and so he had continued fasting and self-flagellation. And he claimed to see visions. In one five-hour trance he saw the world writhing in pestilence and death. He awoke bathed in sweat that stung the open wounds on his back. With these visions, his preaching moved from moral instruction, to earnest warning, to passionate denunciations.

One Sunday, for their perversions and abuses of the weak, he pointed his bony finger and threatened his congregation with misery and damnation in hell. His thundering voice, his fist pounding on the pulpit, rang like a harbinger of doom. At first his congregation sat mesmerized with beads of sweat on their foreheads. What happened to the meek-mannered friar who could barely utter his own name?

In a short time, his people began responding to the divine message. His people in Lombardy cried out for mercy as the people of Connecticut would two hundred and fifty years later, when Jonathan Edwards preached *Sinners in the Hands of an Angry God*. This was revival, and word of Savonarola's preaching scattered like seeds on the wind. Eager to avoid the wrath to come, simple folks came in droves to hear the passionate Dominican friar preach repentance from sin and damnation.

Severe as Savonarola's message appears to modern ears, his words were motivated by tenderness for the plight of the lost in his growing flock. And converts abounded. As news of the revival spread, Savonarola received a worried letter from his mother in Ferrara. Fearful that he might be verging on the insane, she implored him to calm down and return home, if only for a visit. He wrote back:

> *I have renounced this world and devoted myself to working the vineyard of the Lord in various cities to save not only my own soul but those of others as well. If the Lord has given me a talent, I must use it as he pleases; and since he has chosen me for this holy office, be content that I exercise it outside*

my own country, for here, I bear far greater fruit than in Ferrara.

'A prophet is not without honour except in his home town' (Mark 6:4), Jesus had said. And so Savonarola believed about his ministry. So he set out to preach and evangelize anywhere but in his home town: Milan, Venice, Padua, other northern Italian cities — but not Ferrara.

Savonarola's preaching drew more attention and more listeners. After hearing him preach against worldly ambition, wealthy Florentine philosopher Pico della Mirandola stepped into the warm Italian sunshine, musing soberly on what he had heard. It was not the most eloquent delivery, but there was conviction and truth in the friar's words.

Mirandola was himself frustrated with the hypocrisy, moral laxity and tyranny of the Roman Church, and in Savonarola and his preaching he began to see a possible avenue of reform. What is more, Mirandola had friends in high places in Florence, notably Lorenzo de Medici, 'The Magnificent', as he liked being called. Through Mirandola's influence, Savonarola was called back to San Marco in 1489.

Wealth and trade

Wealthy Florence in Savonarola's time was one of the leading trading centres in Europe. Encouraged by Medici rule and modelled by their extravagant lifestyle, silk, spices, precious gems, rugs and dyes flowed over the Silk Road from China to the streets, houses and pockets of Florence. Extravagant material prosperity was on display in the lavish houses and furnishings, in the art and architecture, in the clothing and fashions, and in the hedonistic lifestyle that so inevitably springs from burgeoning temporal wealth.

The Republic of Florence was located well inland from the Liguria Sea, but its borders extended to the ocean, forming a hook in the Italian boot. Common to all Italian city-states was the problem of the smaller principalities within their dominions itching to get out from under the major city's yoke. For Florence, Pisa was the itching principality.

Splendid place that it is even today, Florence when Savonarola arrived this second time was a powder keg in a smoking parlour, on the verge of igniting from political, commercial and artistic rivalries. Arguably, Savonarola could not have landed in a more volatile situation. But it was the precise situation that needed his message so desperately.

4

Lorenzo the Magnificent

With a mere stroke of the quill from the Medicis the Dominicans scrambled to bring Savonarola back to Florence early in 1489. Though the city on the Arno River called itself a republic, Lorenzo ran the show. Eager for his new assignment, Savonarola kept up a steady walking pace through rolling hills and past the budding vineyards of Tuscany. It could have been a delightful journey, with stops for picnicking along the way; but Savonarola had brought no food and water. After fasting the entire distance, he collapsed on the dirt road before the high wooden gates of Florence.

As his new brothers from San Marco splashed cool water on his face, he muttered, 'During my journey I was upheld by a voice saying, "Remember to do what God bids you to do."' Through familiar streets he was carried, smelling the rich fare and seeing the people adorned in the latest silks and satins of Italian fashion. Repulsed by the rampant commercialism, the obsession with worldly attainments, the love of luxury on every street corner, Savonarola began to grasp why God had called him to this place.

At the rugged doors of the convent he met the prior who gladly assisted him past the cloister and to the stairs that led up to the friars' living quarters. Ascending the steps his eyes would have feasted on Fra Angelico's splendid fresco, *The Annunciation*, arguably his finest work. Down a narrow corridor, under high wooden trusses, he was shown his new quarters, cells that shared a common wall with the church sanctuary. Exhausted, he was laid in bed in full view of another Fra Angelico fresco. Lovely though the painting was, it reminded him to whom the monastery was indebted.

Lorenzo de Medici

Florence was Lorenzo de Medici. Born three years before Savonarola, he was heir to the wealth of Florence's first family. For nearly a century the Medicis had reaped riches from their cloth empire and rolled the fortunes into their international banks. Lorenzo was grandson to the great Cosimo de Medici who had done so much for the city and for God — so he hoped. The family had bankrolled the elaborate refurbishing of San Marco, embellishing its walls with the finest Renaissance frescos.

When Lorenzo was fifteen years old, Cosimo had died leaving Lorenzo's weak father in charge of the family fortunes. Like Chicago in the 1920s, the mob syndicate forced Lorenzo to quickly get savvy with the messy side of organized crime. A rival family, smelling an opportunity to exploit Cosimo's death, tried to rub out the new Godfather during a trip through the country. With keen eyes Lorenzo read the plan and steered his father clear of the ambush. Afterward, the grateful patriarch did still more to lavish on his son a classical education fit for a prince, and that gave him a great love of art and literature.

When his time came, Lorenzo would lavish his patronage and wealth on Florentine artists and scholars. He was intensely loyal to his family; it was expected that he would be so. When told to break tradition and marry a Roman bride, instead of a local girl, he did. Wealth has its privileges, but also its obligations. Besides, most of the Medici banks were in Rome.

In 1469, when Savonarola was attending college in Bologna, Lorenzo's father died, propelling Lorenzo into dual headship of the family along with his brother, Giuliano. Lorenzo was not yet twenty-one and had been married only six months. The brothers made things work but, like snakes in the grass, neighbouring families and states, always polite in public but deadly in darkness, snatched a chunk of territory along the border of Florence.

Lorenzo and the Signoria, the governing body of Florence, hit back by quickly mobilizing a small army of mercenaries. After a Renaissance blitzkrieg, the disputed turf was back in Medici control and paying tribute to the family. Florentines began to gain confidence in their brother rulers.

Lorenzo held no official government office; it was the Medici way. Why be a politician when you could simply control the system through intimidation, bribes and back-alley knifings?

The city

Yet the elected government was not just a façade; it consisted of representatives from the city's twenty-one trade guilds. These guilds were broken into two groups: the upper-crust lawyers, wool and silk merchants, and the lower-tiered sellers of spices, dyes and medicines. The rich families of Florence made sure their preferred men were in the Signoria because Lorenzo's web of legislative and executive councils could, by intrigue and subterfuge, be influenced. Predictably, the conversation of the population of 40,000 was usually business or politics. Shrewd and shifty, they talked with sharp polished tongues and constantly schemed to advance family businesses.

Some of these people ran the seventy banks which funded the lavish fashion and cloth industry that made Florence the Park Avenue of Europe. Strategically placed to get the best wool prices from northern Italy, and silk and cotton from the Far East and Middle East, fabrics were worked by tailors in new ways and new combinations: loose woven muslins intertwined with silk and gold, and taffeta. Florence was synonymous with high fashion, which spawned many other flourishing industries that added to the city's fortunes: jewellers, perfumers, cobblers, knitters, and needle and scissor makers.

Political intrigue

Secure in the family's power from within, Lorenzo knew that trouble threatened his rule from other quarters. Pope Sixtus

IV seethed with anger from his seat in Rome. His constant scheming to expand his family's wealth and influence had depleted Papal State reserves. Also, the Vatican needed to be chic, and the pope had his own pet art projects. But when he asked the Medicis for a loan, they had denied him. A broke pope was less apt to be a nuisance. Besides, Lorenzo had treaties with Milan and Venice to stand against the expansionist Papal State.

Then in 1478, while the ruling Medici brothers knelt for communion, an assassination attempt was made on their lives. Giuliano died of multiple stab wounds. Lorenzo's bloody clothes were torn off and a single slash was stitched shut. Now the sole Medici ruler, Lorenzo was pretty sure he knew who was responsible. He ordered swift revenge. By nightfall the bodies of eighty agents of the offended pope slept with the fish.

Promptly excommunicating Lorenzo, the pope declared war and ordered the Republic to hand over the brigand. Papal armies, attired in clothes made by Florentine mills, marched against Florence. But the Medici power base was strong, and the citizens assured Lorenzo of their fealty by writing to the pope:

> You say that Lorenzo is a tyrant and command us to expel him. But most of us Florentines call him their defender. Remember your high office as Vicar of Christ. Remember that the keys of Saint Peter were not given to you to abuse in such a way. Florence will resolutely defend her liberties, trusting in Christ who knows the justice of her cause, and who does not desert those who believe in Him; trusting

in her allies who regard her cause as their own; especially
trusting in the most Christian King, Louis of France, who has
ever been the patron and protector of the Florentine state.

Florence's allegiance with France and her flagrant defying of
the pope would come back to haunt them and Savonarola
in the years ahead. For two years war and hardship ground
down Lorenzo and his loyalists, but the pope's southern
allies lost interest in the war. Behind the pope's back
Lorenzo negotiated with his ally, the King of Naples. It came
at a price, but peace was restored to the Republic. The war-
weary people of Florence awarded Lorenzo the title, *The*
Magnificent.

In 1484, while Savonarola was preaching in Lombardy,
the pope died. Lorenzo quickly made friends with his
replacement, Innocent III. Famous for burning witches, the
pope married his eldest son — yes, popes had sons — to
Lorenzo's daughter. The arrangement obtained a Cardinal's
hat for Lorenzo's thirteen-year-old son Giovanni who would
eventually become Martin Luther's rival, Pope Leo X (1475–
1521).

Peace and new treaties returned prosperity, and Lorenzo
immersed himself in the arts. He established a school for
young artists and invited an upcoming artistic genius to be
raised with his kids. His name was Michelangelo Buonarroti
(1475–1564).

By the time Savonarola burst on the scene, Lorenzo's character
was set. Tolerant but sceptical, he surrounded himself with
men who admired the Bible as poetry and laughed at their

prince's lewd attempts at verse. Moral laxity and a sceptical spirit produced satirical literature lampooning everything of value. Attracted by rich endowments and the freedom to paint pagan subject matter, Sandro Botticelli (1445–1510) arrived in Florence in 1485 and joined the revelry. A favourite of Lorenzo's, he earlier painted the *Primavera* and would soon paint *Birth of Venus*, two paintings that would typify the spirit of the age.

Savonarola and Lorenzo

This was the world into which Savonarola had been dropped. At the monastery of San Marco, Savonarola regained strength. Picking up where he left off years before, he taught novices, but now with vigour and skill. He spoke with zeal and conviction, and felt a renewed confidence in God's calling on his life. Within weeks, attendance at his classes increased so much that Savonarola had to teach his novices out under the hot sun in the roomy cloister.

Pleased with his new friar, on 1 August 1489 the prior invited Savonarola to preach. After careful preparation he ascended the steps to the pulpit. Sweat broke on his forehead as he recalled the preaching disasters that were his last sermons in Florence. The blistering Mediterranean summer heat didn't make matters any better.

Torn by the theatrical training he had received, and the straightforward call of God on his life, he opened the Scriptures and read out his text. Then with zeal and authority, he expounded the sacred words, applying them forcefully on his flock. As he progressed through his sermon, he became more passionate, more vociferous, more animated. At first the congregation sat still in wonder, riveted by his words. More and more, the meaning of what he was proclaiming pricked their hearts. The chapel rang with tears and wailing. He had learned the craft of an evangelist. Every time Savonarola preached, more Florentines came back to hear him.

Perhaps because of the newness of his calling, Savonarola avoided condemning specific individuals — that would come later. Instead, he confronted the congregation with threats of divine wrath if they continued their present course of luxurious living and destructive gossip. With the people begging for hope and forgiveness he told them of Christ's work on the cross. Before his feet, as the peasants in Lombardy had done, the citizens begged forgiveness. And a revival of a sort began. But this was sophisticated Florence, educated and sceptical; not everyone was revived by his preaching. When he came down from the pulpit, his enemies pounced.

'You're mad,' one man yelled. The man proceeded to rant at the preacher, giving out all the details of his madness. Looking calmly into the red face of his accoster, Savonarola listened quietly, then in a soft voice assured him he was in full possession of all his wits. The humanist dismissed him with the condescension of a college professor, assuming he was a poorly educated friar. But Savonarola replied in perfect Latin and parried the objections with informed reasoning: 'Your Aristotle does not even succeed in proving the immortality of the soul; he remains uncertain about points so capital that I do not understand how you can waste so much labour on his pages.' Of Plato he said, 'A simple old woman knows more of the true faith.' Next he would turn on the Renaissance humanists and their worship of ancient manuscripts:

> *Some have so fettered themselves and surrendered their intelligence to the bondage of the ancients that they will say nothing contrary to their customs or that they have not said. If the ancients have not said something, you think we must not say it. If the ancients have done a beautiful deed, are we not to do it also?*

Though he bested them, Savonarola knew they would lick their wounds and return. But the general public in Florence loved it.

Arriving to preach on Sunday, he found vast crowds waiting. Once again he would give them the dismal message of law and the wrath of God. Turn from that wrath, or judgement awaits. Nobody could deliver the bad news better than Savonarola. One man attempting to copy down what Savonarola preached said, 'I was overcome by weeping and could not go on.'

But Savonarola had a growing understanding of the good news of the gospel of grace. Mercifully, when all seemed lost, he would point them to God's mercy through the justifying and finished work of Christ on the cross. One listener gave us a description of his preaching and its effect on his listeners:

> *The promptness of his speech, the lofty grandeur of his themes, the grace of his phrases, his clear and penetrating*

voice, his face not merely fervent but full of enthusiasm, and
beautiful gestures, pierced the hearts of the hearers so they
were not only wrapped in attention but transported beyond
themselves.

Congregations of up to 12,000 souls packed the nave of the
cathedral under Brunelleschi's Dome.

When he preached, it was as if Savonarola soared to the
heavens, finding food and strength of which others know
nothing. But when he finished a sermon, the exertion on
his body, weakened by fasting and flagellation, left him
exhausted. His admiring Dominican brothers doted on him,
and then got him ready for the next bout.

'Remember to do what God bids you to do,' he would recall
back in the quiet of his cell. Till now he had yet to attack
the sins of public figures, like Lorenzo or members of the
Signoria, or corrupt bishops or the pope. Deep in his heart
he knew that there was much more for him to do in the
pulpit. But though he knew it would come at a price, he
vowed to attack the root of the enemy in his lair.

5

Stirring the pot

During the winter of 1491, while Columbus was petitioning Ferdinand and Isabella to fund his westward voyage of discovery, Savonarola was elected prior of San Marco. It was customary for such an honour to be followed by a courtesy visit to the ruling Medici family. Instead, Savonarola skipped the visit. 'I recognize my election as coming from God alone,' he said, 'and to him I will profess obedience.'

His patron brushed off the offence — for the moment — and continued making San Marco more an art museum than a monastery. Art enthusiasts daily came to the monastery to 'gawk' at the paintings, elbowing their way around hooded friars at their prayers.

Savonarola's highest priority was restoring the monastery to God and his work. He promptly sold many of the art treasures of San Marco and organized the friars into manual labourers and tradesmen to help replace the lost revenue from museum admission fees. Friars of San Marco roamed the back roads of Tuscany, the tradesmen teaching and the manual labourers earning money for the monastery. Next, Savonarola reformed the rules of the order, and sent the friars back to studying God's Word and to praying and fasting. Moreover, he restored the ban on ownership of private property, reinstituted the rule of silence, and replaced their designer habits crafted by Florentine tailors with coarse homespun robes. Dozens of new recruits flocked to him, and the convent's population swelled to 250 brothers.

Savonarola was unable to sell all the artwork at San Marco. Before the new prior's arrival, Dominican friar Fra Angelico had decorated the cells of the monks' cloister with magnificent frescoes. Savonarola worried that these were distractions to the friars in their study and meditation, but painting over them was out of the question; the public outcry would destroy him. So he considered abandoning San Marco for a cloister in the Tuscan countryside. Agreeable to the younger brothers, the idea enraged the senior friars who threatened rebellion.

San Marco was ruled by the Lombard Congregation of Convents from Milan, but Savonarola feared they were too corrupt to hear his appeal. Clandestinely, he twice visited the Dominican General in Venice, while sending his most trusted subordinate, Fra Domenico, to make their appeal in Rome. Autonomy for San Marco was their plea. When the Lombard authorities found out, they were furious. Then help came from an unexpected quarter. No real fan of Savonarola, but intractable rival of the Lombard authorities in Milan, Piero de Medici stepped in. He influenced his younger brother Giovanni, now a cardinal, to appeal to the pope.

In the thick of the haggling, Savonarola wrote to Domenico: 'Be strong, do not doubt. Victory will be yours: the Lord scatters the schemes of men and casts down the designs of princes.' He also sent a petition that included all the names of the friars in San Marco and assured Domenico they were all praying.

And God heard their prayers. An influential cardinal cared little for the corrupt Dominican authorities in Milan. After days of closed-door negotiations, the pope signed a bill making San Marco independent, answerable only to those who had brokered the deal. A handful of convents in neighbouring cities joined the newly reorganized San Marco monastery.

The gloves come off

By the spring of 1491, Savonarola felt growing conviction about his preaching; he felt he needed to be more direct, and to confront sin and vanity with less restraint. Florence was a city that prided itself on its beauty, but Savonarola was unconvinced. Perhaps he had been meditating on Proverbs 11:22 that morning: 'Like a gold ring in a pig's snout is a beautiful woman without discretion.' In any event, he launched his opening salvo at the vanity of women:

> Ye women, who glory in your ornaments, your hair, your hands, I tell you, you are all ugly. Would you see true beauty?

Look at the pious man or woman in whom spirit dominates matter; watch him when he prays, when a ray of the divine beauty glows upon him when his prayer is ended; you will see the beauty of God shining in his face, you will behold it as it were the face of an angel.

But this was only the beginning. It was the vain and corrupt friars, monks and priests who bore greater responsibility. And so he levelled his guns on the clergy. His words may have had more effect on the hearts of laymen who heard and saw all about them the truth of what he declared. 'In these days there is no grace, no gift of the Holy Spirit that may not be bought or sold. The poor are oppressed by grievous burdens, and when they are called to pay sums beyond their means, the rich cry unto them, "Give me the rest."'

A lesser pastor would have catered to the rich: they were the patrons of monasteries; they were the influential ones; they were the ones that could be allies of a reforming preacher. But Savonarola never calculated his message, never shaped it to gain advantage, never genuflected for favours from anyone.

There be some who, having an income of fifty a year, pay a tax on one hundred, while the rich pay little, since the taxes are regulated at their pleasure. Bethink ye well, O ye rich, for affliction shall smite ye. This city shall no more be called Florence but a den of thieves, of baseness and bloodshed. Then shall ye all be poverty-stricken and your name, O priests, shall be changed into a terror.

Calling their city a 'den of thieves' was an affront to the wealthy, but Savonarola pressed on, firing a second broadside at those who controlled the financial industry, so central to the Florentine economy:

> *You have found many ways of making money, and many exchanges which you call lawful but which are most unjust; and you have corrupted the offices and magistrates of the city. No one can persuade you that usury is sinful; you defend it at the peril of your souls. No one is ashamed of lending at usury; nay, those who do otherwise pass for fools. Your brow is that of a whore, and you will not blush. You say, a good and glad life lies in gain; and Christ says, 'blessed are the poor in spirit, for they shall inherit heaven.'*

Few preachers in the history of the church have been so uncompromisingly forthright. Savonarola's new resolves for his preaching extended still further. For the political ruler of Florence, Lorenzo de Medici, who had done so much for San Marco, yet who would go down in history as a quintessential tyrant, he had this to say:

> *Tyrants are incorrigible because they are proud, because they love flattery, and will not restore ill-gotten gains. They hearken not unto the poor, and neither do they condemn the rich. They corrupt voters, and farm out taxes to aggravate the burdens of the people. The tyrant is wont to occupy the people with shows and festivals, in order that they may think of their own pastimes and not of his designs, and, growing unused to the conduct of the commonwealth, may leave the reins of government in his hands.*

Smitten by the truth of his words, the people came trembling back for more. And as they listened, many fell to their knees in fear and wept; unmoved critics looked on and called them *Piagnoni*, weepers.

Hearing Savonarola's bold denouncements, many have dismissed him as a harsh, unfeeling preacher. Popular as this conclusion is, it is a deeply flawed one. Tender toward the lost, like a father to the wayward son, he began calling the city, 'My Florence.' Nothing is ultimately more liberating than the truth. Just as Luther told Wittenberg the truth, and Calvin told it to Geneva, and Knox to Edinburgh, so Savonarola declared the truth to Florence, and they loved him for it — for a while.

Trouble brewing

After sermons like these, it takes little imagination to guess the topic of conversation at the Medici palace. Had not Grandfather Cosimo pumped endless money into restoring San Marco? Hadn't he commissioned Fra Angelico to adorn nearly every wall in the monastery with the magnificent frescoes? Why would Savonarola rail on Lorenzo? Rail on other rich people, but why on your patron? It had always been customary for the church to get their digs in on the rich, but this scrawny friar was stirring up the people and threatening the very foundation of the family power base. Something had to be done.

Meanwhile, Savonarola stuck to his convictions and continued his attacks the very next Sunday:

> *Nor shall that dictatorship be excused on the ground that it finances literature and art. The literature and art are*

> *pagan; the humanists merely pretend to be Christians; those*
> *ancient authors whom they so sedulously exhume and edit*
> *and praise are strangers to Christ and the Christian virtues,*
> *and their art is an idolatry of heathen gods, or a shameless*
> *display of naked women and men.*

Enraged, but cautious, the Medicis attempted appeasement by sending Savonarola expensive presents. It had worked with every other cleric. Maybe lavish gifts would turn his ire on other tyrants; and there were plenty of them. But Savonarola could not be bought. 'A faithful dog', he replied, 'does not leave off barking in his master's defence because a bone is thrown to him.'

Lorenzo altered course and tried a different tack. If personal gifts would not move him, maybe ones earmarked for the monastery would. He placed a large bag of gold florins in the alms box. Wise to the Medici game, Savonarola gifted it to another monastery. 'It is wrong and even wicked for men in holy orders to seek out top bosses', he said, 'because the consequent ties could only end in compromises, lies, and corruption for the servants of God.'

Feeling he had attacked the Medicis enough, he went after the Church again. Since the thirteenth century, when friars or priests took holy orders they could expect comfortable lives. Safe within the cloister walls they bled the faithful and kept them in the dark about the gospel and the way to God. Some would even become the private priests of wealthy patrons and perform private masses for the souls of their clients and dead family members in chapels adorned with the family's coat of arms. Savonarola had words for them:

In these days, prelates and preachers are chained to the earth by the love of earthly things. The care of souls is no longer their concern. They are content with the receipt of revenue. The preachers preach to please princes and to be praised by them. They have done worse. They have not only destroyed the Church of God. They have built up a new Church after their own pattern. Go to Rome and see! In the mansions of the great prelates there is no concern save for poetry and the oratorical art. Go thither and see! Thou shalt find them all with the books of the humanities in their hands and telling one another that they can guide men's souls by means of Virgil, Horace and Cicero.

Clearly, Savonarola knew the Renaissance, and he knew its preference for the authorities of pagan antiquity over the Bible. And he was equally clear on the effect this all had on the poor.

The prelates of former days had fewer gold mitres and chalices and what few they possessed were broken up and given to relieve the needs of the poor. But our prelates, for the sake of obtaining chalices, will rob the poor of their sole means of support. Dost thou not know what I would tell thee! What doest thou, O Lord! Arise, and come to deliver thy Church from the hands of devils, from the hands of tyrants, from the hands of iniquitous prelates.

Enjoying Savonarola's attack on the clergy, Lorenzo courted an alliance with Savonarola by inviting him to preach in the Medici palace. Surely the magnificence of his own home would force his guest to act with constraint and respect.

> *I am here in the waters of Tiberius. Before the signori I do not feel master of myself as in church. I must be more measured and urbane...*

so began Savonarola. Lorenzo may have breathed a sigh of relief and settled back onto his satin couch at the words. But Savonarola was not finished:

> *I must be more measured and urbane, as Christ was in the house of the Pharisees. I shall say, therefore, that all the evil of a city depends on its head, whose responsibility is great even for small sins, for if he followed the right path the whole city would become holy.*

Standing on Lorenzo's oriental carpets, surrounded by the finest art collection in Florence, breathtaking wealth glittering blindly in his eyes; nevertheless, Savonarola was unimpressed, and proceeded without scruples, speaking still more frankly and openly.

> *Tyrants are incorrigible because they are proud, because they love flattery, because they will not restore ill-gotten gains. They give a free hand to bad officials: they yield to flattery, they do not heed the wretched, they do not condemn the rich; they expect the peasants and the poor to work for them and allow their officials to oppress them. They corrupt the suffrage: they farm the taxes and burden the people more and more.*

Savonarola paused for breath, rounding up on his finale.

It is your duty, therefore, to root out dissension, to do
justice, and to demand honesty of everyone.

Tyrant that he was, with a reputation for decisive cruelty
to any who opposed him, why didn't Lorenzo just take
the troublesome friar out? He had henchmen aplenty for
just such purposes; why not quietly and conveniently be
rid of Savonarola? The reason was becoming clear. Signs
of Lorenzo's failing health were the talk about town. The
dying Godfather was pondering judgement and the world
to come.

Prophetic commission

And then one night in Savonarola's cell, it began. He saw, as
he slept, a sword bearing the inscription, 'Behold the sword
of the Lord will descend suddenly and quickly upon the
earth, split the sky.' He rolled on his side to try and hide his
eyes, but still the vision remained. The sword turned toward
earth and the sky went black. Soaking his covers with sweat,
suddenly he saw light glint off swords and arrows raining
fire down on the earth, on Florence and the surrounding
countryside. It was horrible, and all so real: thunder rocked
the heavens, and famine and death covered the earth. A
voice from heaven commanded him to preach what he had
seen, and the vision vanished. He awoke with a pounding
heart. What else was he to conclude? God was commanding
him to preach, to save Florence from the wrath to come. He
referred to this prophetic vision until his death.

Ironically, Savonarola believed in visions 'beyond the scope
of the knowledge which is natural to any creature.' He firmly

believed he was a prophet, yet he knew the only way to fulfil the commission given in this prophetic vision was to preach the Bible and let the authority of God be known in it. 'I preach the regeneration of the Church,' he said, 'taking the Scriptures as my sole guide.'

Sole guide

Continuationists have little difficulty with this turn of events in Savonarola's ministry; they are confident that the apostolic sign gift of prophesy is still in effect today, so why not in Savonarola's day? Cessationists, however, raise their eyebrows at this point in the unfolding drama of Savonarola's life. Was he a real prophet? Or did his own religious fervour unwittingly augment his dreams and expand his fears of impending doom for corrupt Florence into what he believed were divine revelations?

In Savonarola's work *Manual of Revelations* he wrote that a true prophet would always be sure of God's revelation, would see it fulfilled, knew the results would be for the good, and would be assured by God's faithful people agreeing with it. He believed that his prophecies 'could only be of God because they were consistent with the Scriptures'. They could not be from the devil, as critics accused, because 'Satan hated his sermons and does not know the future.'

Now ceased

The validity of Old Testament prophets was measured by whether what they predicted actually came to pass. Did all of Savonarola's prophecies come to pass? He prophesied political revolution in Florence and that Charles VIII of France would invade Italy. Both came true. He also predicted Florence would recover renegade Pisa — which it did. And he prophesied that Turks and Moors, on an epic scale, would be converted to Christianity. Three out of four is good in basketball but not so good in prophesying. 500 years later, in the Arab Spring of the twenty-first century, we see no immediate signs of mass conversion of the Arab world happening — only the contrary. Christians pray on.

In the opening chapter of the *Westminster Confession of Faith*, 'Of the Holy Scriptures', Puritan divines argued that since the closing of the canon of Scripture, God reveals himself wholly in the written word, 'those former ways of God's revealing his will unto his people being now ceased'.

Well-meaning but ill-informed men like Harold Camping have come along for centuries prophesying that the end of the world and the coming judgement will occur on such and such a date, 'no man knows the day nor the hour' notwithstanding. Yet here we are. The Roman Catholic Church had taught Savonarola that extra-biblical prophecy is still a way God reveals himself; he was naturally a product of that teaching. A shrewd observer of his times, passionate Savonarola was human, like the rest of us, and may have presumed to know more than God intended any of us to know. For this his critics had nothing but scorn.

The contest continues

Lorenzo never recovered from the snub when Savonarola was elected prior but refused to submit to his patronage at San Marco. To Lorenzo it was ungrateful and rude. 'A stranger comes into my house and not even deigns to visit me,' he fumed. In the coming months the two waged nothing short of a war. Lorenzo would look for a chance encounter on the street; Savonarola would politely avoid him.

Frequently, Savonarola was told that Lorenzo was admiring the frescoes and the fragrant gardens of the convent. 'Does he ask for me?' Savonarola would ask. When told that he didn't, Savonarola would respond, 'Then let him walk.' Lorenzo felt if he could just sit down and talk some sense into Savonarola, all would be well.

And still Lorenzo's health grew worse. At last he could no longer come to admire his beloved San Marco. Instead he sent his officials to plead with Savonarola to stop the attacks on the Medici family. Dressed in fine robes and hats that clashed with the plain walls of the convent, the city fathers only strengthened Savonarola's resolve. 'You must moderate your tone,' Lorenzo's messengers threatened, 'or you may bring harm to the convent — and even to yourself.'

'I know you do not come of your own accord,' replied Savonarola, knowing their intentions, 'but that Lorenzo has sent you. Tell him to do penance for his sins, for the Lord fears no one and does not spare the princes of the world.' Further threats fell on empty ears. Three days later Savonarola publicly predicted the death of the King of Naples, of Pope Innocent VIII, and of Lorenzo Medici.

Roiling in rage, Lorenzo called veteran priest, Fra Mariano, Savonarola's old preaching nemesis. Usurped by Savonarola, Mariano had been itching for the opportunity to hit back.

With Lorenzo present, sitting pale and gaunt in his robes of state, Mariano preached from Acts 1:7: 'It is not for you to know times or seasons that the Father has fixed by his own authority.' The scheme to discredit Savonarola backfired. Instead of his famous smooth delivery, Mariano's temper bested him. Slashing the air wildly with his hands, he raged against Savonarola till he had to gulp for air. Mariano's admirers stared in horror at the display.

To Lorenzo's frustration, Savonarola's popularity soared. He got the last word — for the time being. 'Although I am a stranger in the city, and Lorenzo the first man in the state, yet shall I stay here and it is he who will go hence.'

Lorenzo's deathbed

Defeated by the friar, Lorenzo's health failed. Hours before his death, according to the medical wisdom of the day, his physician resorted to feeding him a concoction of crushed gems. It had no effect; it was time for Lorenzo to be honest with himself. Bidding farewell to friends and family, he gasped out final counsel to Piero, his eldest son.

This side of death, the sacraments of absolution and extreme unction were all that remained for Lorenzo to receive. Consisting of final confession, the Eucharist, and an anointing, the Church claimed that these acts would absolve him of any sin since his last confession and prepare him to see Christ. The Medici family priest was within reach and ready to do his duty, but Lorenzo asked for Savonarola. 'I know of no honest friar save that one,' he gasped.

Summoned, Savonarola came to the bedside of the dying tyrant. Gazing about the lavish halls of the Medici palace, he may have frowned at costly tapestries and ancient sculpture lining the walls, praying for wisdom. Savonarola strode up to the massive bed and looked on the sunken features of Lorenzo, his pallid face blending with his pillows. Their eyes locked. Lorenzo said he had three sins to confess. Savonarola listened patiently. Struggling for breath, the dying man asked forgiveness for sacking a city, for robbing a wealthy patron's belongings, and for his ruthless reprisals after the murder of his brother.

Savonarola acknowledged them, and Lorenzo waited expectantly for absolution. Suspicious of Lorenzo's sincerity, Savonarola wanted to get at the heart of the man. He gave him three conditions for absolution. His life ebbing from him, Lorenzo anxiously agreed to hear them. 'First, you must have a strong faith in God's mercy.' The dying man nodded. 'The second is you must tell your sons to restore all ill-gotten wealth.' Again he nodded. Savonarola paused: 'You must instruct your sons to give Florence back her liberties.'

Lorenzo stared hard-eyed at the friar. Silently, he turned his face to the wall. Savonarola hesitated then withdrew without giving absolution. Hours later, 8 April 1492, Lorenzo the Magnificent, the tyrant of Florence, passed into the presence of his Maker, before whom earthly titles and possessions count for nothing.

Critics of Savonarola cite this episode as an example of his harsh, unfeeling character. Not so. Savonarola knew that there was no bargaining with the Judge of the universe.

Savonarola did not want anyone clinging to false hopes of self-salvation, leastwise, Lorenzo. So he wanted to sift out whether Lorenzo was truly repentant or just playing yet another manipulative game — this one with God.

God only knows if after Savonarola left the room, in Lorenzo's final moments, the dying tyrant cried out to Jesus for mercy. But certainly, had Savonarola given him false hope by absolution, presuming on mercy, he would have felt no desperate need for the blood and righteousness of Jesus alone for his eternal salvation.

When through the streets of Florence word spread that Lorenzo was dead, and Savonarola refused to give him absolution, Savonarola's popularity skyrocketed.

6

French invasion

His father's body was still warm when Piero, eldest son of Lorenzo, took over as Godfather of Florence. He was twenty-two. Of all Lorenzo's sons, Piero was the least qualified. Tall, handsome, and a natural athlete, he loved horses, fancy clothes, and playing football with his tunic off. Unlike most Medicis he lacked the unassuming character of his father who had always followed the advice of Cosimo:

> *Do not appear to give advice, but put your views forward discreetly in conversation. Be wary of going to the* Palazzo della Signoria; *wait to be summoned, and when you are summoned, do what you are asked to do, and never display any pride should you receive a lot of votes. Avoid litigation and political controversy, and always keep out of the public eye.*

Savonarola had seen through the ruse as through a ladder, but the manipulative strategy behind these tactics left most everyone else awed with their prince, and it gave his subjects the vague impression they had meaningfully participated in the political process.

But Piero didn't get it. His harsh and haughty displays incited resentment at the beginning and loss of support at the end. When cautioned by advisors in his government, he petulantly brushed off advice, impulsively issuing his own schemes, often resulting in public blunders. When his failures were too great to conceal, he made absurd excuses or pointed the finger at others.

After a few months of bungling, weary of the advice and scolding of his elders, he cut off the wiser counsellors in his court. Like Rehoboam of Israel, he sought the counsel of his young friends and did what they advised. The result was predictably disastrous. Oddly, he continued the family patronage of San Marco despite Savonarola's reforms.

Unfortunately for Piero, storm clouds building to the north were about to throw the young prince into the ring with political heavyweights bent on destroying him.

Political intrigue

Meanwhile, Savonarola kept preaching. But the corrupt machinations of power in Italian politics churned out schemes that would create significant factors in his life and ministry in Florence.

The first of these factors began in 1489 when Pope Innocent VIII (1432–1492) cut a deal with King Charles VIII (1470–1498) of France, giving him the Kingdom of Naples. After ransacking his heritage for any scrap of Italian connection, Charles had generously concluded that through connections on his father's mother's side, most of southern Italy really ought to be his. Elated at his good fortune, the nineteen-year-old king brokered alliances with former enemies, England and Austria, and commenced building his army.

Two years into Charles VIII's scheming, Innocent VIII died. He left behind a depleted treasury, the ashes of thousands of witches he had burned, and enough illegitimate offspring to fill a convent. At the helm of the Eternal City was Rodrigo Borgia, Pope Alexander VI (1431–1503).

Short and fat, greedy and ambitious, clever and charming, the new Spaniard pope had spent the last several years as Vice-Chancellor of the Church, a position second only to the papacy. Ambitious to advance the Borgia family, he would eventually die of malaria, leaving behind a trail of the bodies and souls of his many adversaries. Being Spanish, he had no tolerance for a French army on Italian soil. With blatant disregard for papal supremacy — at least the supremacy of his predecessor — Alexander VI flip-flopped papal policy and issued a bull barring Charles VIII and his French army from the whole of Italy. Young and ambitious, Charles ignored the decree and continued preparing for his invasion.

Judgement on the wicked

Meanwhile, Savonarola grew more distressed at the continued immorality of the Florentines. Early in 1494, he had had enough. Warning his congregation that the sins and debauchery of all Italy would soon be avenged, he prophesied that a glorious reform of the church would come — and that he would die a violent death.

Filled with zeal, Savonarola pounded on the pulpit, further warning that Charles VIII will 'come across the Alps against Italy like Cyrus'. He welcomed the invasion as the inevitable chastening hand of God for the sins of Florence. A listener wrote that Savonarola's sermons were 'so full of terrors and alarms, cries and lamentations, that everyone went about the city bewildered, speechless, and, as if half dead'.

War

In the summer of 1494, Charles VIII's army crossed the French Savoy and arrived at Asti on the Lombard plains west of Milan. After resupplying, his army marched south. Banners inscribed with *Voluntas Dei*, 'The Will of God', snapped in the breeze. Clearly he had convinced himself that this was a holy war and God was on his side.

Charles did not intend to engage in war with the northern Italian city-states; he did, however, need to pass through their territory so he could assert his claims in Naples. There has never been in the history of the world a mass movement of armies without great cost to the people on whose territory those armies pass through. Long before tin cans or Ready-Made Meals, Charles's hungry army — 40,000 strong — left behind them a swathe of trampled fields, empty barns, and dry wells. Those who survived would die of starvation in the months ahead.

Worse still, Charles's army was organized. Made up of crack Swiss mercenaries, Scottish archers, and French heavy cavalry, their most destructive feature was Charles's state-of-the-art artillery. New to European battlefields, the invaders brought scores of cannons, some so large they required six axles and a dozen horses to transport them. Additionally, many of his soldiers were armed with the *arquebus* capable of firing a lead ball 200 yards. Italians melted with fear.

Neither Florence nor any other city-state had such an army so well accoutred for war and destruction. Surely this was the sword that Savonarola had seen poised over Florence in his vision. Florentines knew their geography well enough to know that their fair city lay dead centre in the invasion path.

Confronted with this tsunami of war, the combined Italian army did what they could; they fell back. Accustomed to local squabbles with much lower stakes, the men of Naples, Venice, Milan, Florence and the papal states were determined to avoid pitched battle with such a foe.

But if the Italians would not fight him in respectable combat, Charles was determined to smash everything in sight with his heavy cannons. Castle after castle he pounded into rubble with his artillery. The Italian cause seemed lost.

Dread in Florence

Running ahead of the invading army like cockroaches were scores of refugees, who poured into Florence as harbingers of doom. '*Siamo perduti!*' they cried. 'We are ruined!' Dread of the invasion sent all Florence to the churches, there to seek comfort, to find hope. In September 1494, Savonarola stepped into the pulpit at the Duomo, as many as 12,000 terrified faces turning to him for that hope. 'Behold, the sword has come upon you,' he cried. 'The prophecies are fulfilled, the scourge begun! Behold these hosts are led of the Lord! O Florence, the time of singing and dancing is at an end. Now is the time to shed floods of tears for thy sins.'

Dread mounted as the hours passed. The French army marching ever nearer, he called out to his people, 'This will be your final destruction.' They remembered his earlier prophesies: the death of Innocent VIII, the death of Lorenzo, and now the invasion of the French army. All had come to pass as Savonarola had foretold. Many cried out in repentance. He preached on: hell would soon be filled with Florentines gnashing their teeth, pulling their hair, and digging at oozing sores covering their bodies. With Piero and his youthful officials impotent and on the ropes, Savonarola preached one of his most terrifying sermons:

> Rethink you well, O ye rich, for affliction shall smite ye. This city shall no more be Florence, but a den of thieves, of turpitude and bloodshed. Then shall ye all be poverty-stricken, all wretched, and your name, O priests, shall be changed into a terror. Know that unheard-of times are at hand.

Negotiations and schemes

By early October, the terror had begun. Charles' army entered Florentine territory and besieged the fortress of Sarzana. With little hope of success, Piero de Medici, far less than magnificent, rode out to meet the invaders in the hope of negotiating an honourable settlement.

Scrawny Charles, greatly the physical inferior of Piero, but greatly his superior in political acumen, made outrageous demands on the young Medici prince. He knew that Piero was on thin ice with the Signoria and had nothing to counter his demands. So he held out. At last Piero conceded to all Charles's demands: free passage guaranteed for the invading army; two strategic bastions in western Florence, including Pisa with its leaning bell tower, and more were to be surrendered. To top off his demands, Charles charged Florence 200,000 florins to help fund his war.

The terms were carried ahead of the returning delegation by fast courier. When the Florentine city government read the concessions, they were enraged. Piero had rendered up everything. Should they not have been consulted? Despite the power-grabbing of the Medicis in the past, they had always been consulted, or at least kept informed. Plans to depose Piero had simmered in the Signoria; now the time had come. They must cast off Medici rule and restore the republic.

Medici fall

Hours later, when Piero entered the gates of Florence, there was no grand procession to greet him. On the contrary, people jeered and threw stones. He thought he had saved them and tried to explain, but when he found the gates of the *Palazzo Vecchio* locked — Florence had locked him out of his own city hall — he knew he was ruined.

Spurring his horse back to the palace, Piero frantically rounded up his family and fled. After breaking down the front gate, the angry citizenry stomped through the manicured gardens, yanking up shrubs and smashing hedges.

Beating down the door of the castle, they began tearing down curtains, wrecking furniture and stuffing their tunics with silver and fine china. In a matter of hours, four generations of Medicis had been tossed out and their art collection plundered. The Signoria offered a 5,000-florin reward for Piero and his brother Giovanni alive, 2,000 florins for them dead. Disgraced, the Medicis fled north to Bologna.

Savonarola negotiates

Meanwhile, Charles VIII still awaited the fulfilment of his demands agreed upon by now-deposed Piero de Medici. Though the Signoria still had a crisis on their hands, one thing was clear: Savonarola's prophecy of God's judgement against Florence was unfolding. 'If he could predict the invasion,' the Signoria now reasoned, 'maybe he could appease the French king and work out a deal.' A delegation was formed to renegotiate peace with Charles, and Savonarola was made a delegate. Once again, he stepped into his pulpit:

> The Lord has heard your prayers. He has brought about a great revolution peaceably. He alone, when everyone else abandoned it, has come to the aid of the city. Persevere, O people of Florence, in good works, persevere in peace. If you wish the Lord to persevere in mercy, be merciful to your brothers, your friends, your enemies, otherwise you will feel the scourges being prepared. Woe to him who breaks his commandments.

Six officials from the Signoria, Savonarola among them, rode
out to meet Charles VIII and his conquering army. At Pisa
they were met by a citizenry more hostile to them than were
the invaders. Free of their Florentine chains, the people of Pisa
were hailing the French as liberators. With feigned courtesy,
Charles brought Savonarola and the delegation before him.
Negotiations began. Savonarola told the king in French, 'You
are an instrument sent by the Lord to relieve Italy of its woes
and to reform the Church.' Unimpressed, the king remained
resolute. Next, in a strategy of desperation, the Florentines
demanded recognition of their independence and the return
of Pisa after the war. It seemed laughable. Meanwhile, the
French had their invincible army. So it seemed.

What Savonarola and the delegation did not know was
that Charles's supply lines were dwindling, with the supply
from Bordeaux now all but dried up. Just as Englishmen let
nothing come between them and their tea, so the French
would eventually be unwilling to pursue a campaign that cut
them off from their wine.

Charles VIII kept his problems to himself, and ended the
negotiations noncommittally; he would let them know
his decision when he arrived with his army in Florence. It
looked like failure for the delegation — and for Florence.

The French enter Florence

In late October word arrived in Florence that Charles VIII's
army had brutally sacked the Florentine town of Fivizzano.
All Florence was paralyzed with dread; Fivizzano was but

seventy miles away. In mid-November, emissaries of the French army arrived in Florence, strolling through the best neighbourhoods marking homes for billeting troops. Florentines' hearts sank. On 17 November 1494, Charles VIII's army arrived at their gates. By nightfall Charles had billeted himself in the Medici mansion. When he learned that Piero de Medici had fled, impressed with Savonarola at Pisa, he asked for the prior of San Marco to be brought to him. Word on the streets was that Savonarola was the only person in Florence who really understood what was going on.

'Your coming has lightened our hearts,' said Savonarola to Charles, 'exhilarated our minds, inasmuch as God has sent you.' Italians may have thought Savonarola's words sounded like treason, but he had more to say to the invading king:

> Therefore, most Christian king, listen carefully to my words and bind them to your heart. Be merciful, especially with Florence, where God has many servants, despite its sins. Guard and defend the innocents — widows, orphans, the wretched and above all the chastity of the women's convents. God elected you in the interest of the church. You must obey the Lord.

It was a bold move and bravely done. And it worked. Charles and his army marched out of Florence on 28 November 1494. People danced for joy in the streets. Savonarola had saved their city.

With both the Medicis and the King of France now gone, the entire city turned to Girolamo Savonarola to lead it to democracy.

7

New republic

Only weeks had passed since the flight of Piero de Medici, but already the people were restless for change. The Signoria and its ruling councils were tentatively in place, but any official who wanted to keep his office knew he had better act — and act fast.

On 2 December 1494, the great bell in the tower of the *Palazzo Vecchio* called the people to the plaza at its base. Under the watchful eye of guards armed with pikes and muskets, people poured into the square. Eager to hear what form the new government would take, they pressed forward, straining to hear the chief secretary — and then to cast their vote.

Savonarola was clear about what form that new government ought to take, and he had not been shy in letting his opinion be known:

> The Lord bids you renew everything and destroy the past;
> nothing must remain of our bad laws, our bad habits, and

our bad government. This is a time when words must yield
to facts, and vain ceremonies to true feelings. The Lord has
said, 'I was hungry, and ye gave me meat; I was naked, and
ye clothed me.' He did not say, 'Ye have built me a beautiful
church or a fine convent.' He desires only labours of love;
love must renew all things.

Dressed in his colourful robe of office, the chief secretary of
the Signoria stepped out onto the high balcony of the palace
and read out a four-part bill. Would it reflect Savonarola's
priorities for the city? The first provision annulled existing
laws that conflicted with the new laws. The second provision
abolished the executive and legislative branches of Medici
rule. The third provision permitted all political exiles to
return to Florence. And the fourth provision established a
new transitional commission of twenty men to be appointed
by the old Signoria to help elect new officials.

The council of twenty consisted of the wealthy elite of
Florence, bankers and merchants. For sixty years of Medici
rule they had gained the experience to run the city —
but the Medici way. Some even wanted to bring Piero de
Medici back. The people cried foul, and many shouted for
Savonarola.

Didn't a republic mean the people had more voice in
their government? That was what the citizens of Florence
thought. But the elite council of twenty was reluctant to
relinquish power to the citizens. Haggling erupted, and
soon the machinery of the interim government broke down.
Merchants and tradesmen, disgusted with the political
logjam, took their businesses elsewhere. Unemployment

mounted. Angry crowds gathered in the streets. Desperate, the interim Signoria summoned Savonarola.

Holy City

'I will preach, but why need I meddle with the government of Florence?' Savonarola posed the question in a sermon. He then proceeded to give the Lord's answer to his objections and reluctance: 'If thou wouldst make Florence a holy city, thou must establish her on firm foundations and give her a government which cherishes righteousness.' He concluded his sermon by arguing that a democracy founded on the Bible was the only sound government for sinful people.

After the sermon, he invited the Signoria to San Marco and explained his plan to overhaul Florence's government. The new constitution would resemble Venice's, the most stable Italian city-state. Rule by one man was not an option in Savonarola's mind. 'In Italy and, above all in Florence,' he explained, 'where both strength and intellect abound, where men have keen wits and restless spirits, the government of the one can only result in tyranny.'

The problem, as Savonarola saw things, was that 'Men want to be big and rule over everybody.' He therefore argued for a constitution that provided for elected bodies of government: 'It is best then to be ruled over by groups of men.'

Furthermore, Savonarola was certain that no man this side of heaven could rule without checks and balances on his power. The restraint on leaders' power would come from more inclusive voting and broader eligibility for holding political office. He wanted not just wealthy, high-born people in government. He wanted to see artisans and labourers holding political office in Florence.

In a sermon preached at the Duomo, Savonarola declared: 'The will of God is that the city of Florence be ruled by the people and not by tyrants. Let no man contradict this, and if what I have said is not true I am ready to stand before God on the Day of Judgement to render a good account.'

Similar to the constitution in Venice, Savonarola desired a Great Council for Florence, formed of men with political experience. To act as checks on their personal ambitions, the Great Council was divided into three committees holding office for only six alternating months at a time. The Signoria would remain in place and, for the time, complete democracy would have to wait until there was a better educated citizenry in Florence.

'God alone will be thy king, O Florence,' declared Savonarola in a sermon, 'as he was king of Israel under the old Covenant. 'Thy new head shall be Jesus Christ.' Moreover, Savonarola refused to have any seat on the council, choosing rather to serve as the soul of the entire people.

On 23 December 1494, the Great Council was installed. As cumbersome as it sounded it was a great improvement over Medici tyrannies, the middle-class solution to domineering nobles. It would stay in place till 1512 when the Medicis took back Florence in a power-play assisted by the pope. Through Savonarola's leadership the new constitution gained public support, with the new republic officially in operation 10 June 1495.

Moral reform

Since virtue is the foundation of any sound government, Savonarola set about to influence the Great Council to that end. He began with a plan to grant amnesty to supporters of the old regime. The Medicis had made many bitter enemies in Florence. One Florentine wrote that without Savonarola's act of clemency, the streets would have been bathed in blood.

That was just the beginning. Savonarola was determined to develop a fair and equitable taxation in Florence and to provide alternatives to loan sharks who gouged the less affluent with usury. Under Savonarola's influence, interest rates dropped from 30% down to 5%. To help families avoid financial ruin, he also petitioned for laws putting a ceiling on marriage dowries.

Moreover, at Savonarola's urging, the Council also enacted laws forbidding horse races, perverted songs, profanity and gambling. To help enforce these laws, there were rewards for informing against offenders. And convicted offenders could be tortured, blasphemers have their tongues pierced, and habitual homosexuals could be stoned.

'Evil man is a servant to his sins,' preached Savonarola, 'he is not free, and so cannot be a good citizen and can't properly serve his city.' And he helped define what being a good citizen looked like: 'Confess your sins, speak civilly, forgive the Medicis just as God has forgiven you; return pilfered money, and serve the common good not personal advancement.'

In the near future, Savonarola was to discover that not everyone wanted a virtuous society.

8

Soul of Florence

There was no golden age for Savonarola in Florence. The republic was no sooner established than the greedy and ambitious schemed against Savonarola and his influence in their city. Grand Florence, the birthplace of the Renaissance, was now headed by an unsophisticated friar. Medici supporters schemed on one side, jealous Franciscans on another, and the Hedonists on yet another. Savonarola's enemies called his followers *Piagnoni*, weepers, and hypocrites and prayer-munchers. His supporters snapped back, calling Savonarola's critics 'mad dogs'.

Gathering on every street corner were grumblers and gossips, hurling criticism at every new change in their city. What was true and what was rumour was anyone's guess.

But Savonarola had a new tool. In 1471 the first printing press, the brainchild of Johannes Gutenberg (1398–1468), arrived in Florence. While many criticized the new technology, Savonarola saw it as an invaluable ally. In short order, he could print pamphlets, speeches and sermons, and have them available throughout the city. By the end of his life, he was the most published writer of the century.

Hostility shifts

Meanwhile, Charles VIII pressed toward Naples. By December he had plundered Rome, with Pope Alexander VI rendering up his illegitimate son (could popes have any other kind?) for ransom. On 22 February 1495, without a fight, Charles VIII occupied Naples and was crowned its king.

For all his zeal, Savonarola lacked political *savoir faire*. Fearing what the king of France — and now Naples — would do with his new power, he wrote Charles a letter warning that if he harmed Florence: 'God's wrath would be poured out upon [his] head.' In another letter he wrote: 'God has chosen this city and determined to magnify her and raise her up and, whoso touches her, touches the apple of his eye.'

Savonarola was not the only Italian leader worried about Charles and his new powers. Rome, Venice, Milan and the King of Spain formed the Holy League, a coalition to expel Charles. When Florence was urged to join, Savonarola refused. He still maintained that Charles was God's chosen instrument to judge Italy for her sins. Politically speaking, this was an enormous blunder that would come back to haunt Florence.

By spring, Naples had had enough of Charles and forced him out. The Holy League harried his supply lines and engaged in skirmishes as he retreated north. After a bloody battle at Fornovo, Charles managed to escape with the remains of his army. Three years later, he hit his head on a door lintel while playing tennis and died.

Dusting their hands of Charles, the Holy League turned its attention on Florence. For failing to support the Italian campaign to expel Charles from Italy, Savonarola and Florence were now seen as traitors. Hostility mounted from all sides.

Reform continues

Meanwhile, the majority of Florentines accepted Savonarola's moral reforms, the women dressing modestly, and vulgar songs were replaced with hymn-singing. Churches were full, and charitable giving rose to unprecedented levels. Some bankers and merchants even restored profits they had acquired through unethical business tactics. Savonarola continued the reforms and seemed well aware that the real issues went deeper than external changes. Real reform, he knew, 'must begin with the things of the spirit'. To those who wanted the prior of San Marco out of politics, to turn government back over to secular leaders, and to separate church from state, he replied: 'this is the rule of tyrants, a rule for oppressing, not for liberating a city. If you desire a good government you must restore it to God.' He declared that with Christ as their head, 'O Florence! then wilt thou be rich with spiritual and temporal wealth; thou wilt achieve the reformation of Rome, of Italy, of all countries; the wings of thy greatness shall spread over the world.'

Boys of San Marco

Next Savonarola organized the boys of the city, ages twelve to twenty and from all walks of life, into 'The Boys of San Marco'. These boys pledged to attend church regularly, to avoid races, pageants, acrobatic displays, loose company, obscene literature, dancing and music schools, and to wear their hair short. Walking the streets, they solicited alms for the church and dispersed groups participating in activities they had pledged to avoid.

Well meaning as Savonarola was in this, it was a formula for disaster. The misguided plan backfired when some of the boys, in their self-righteous zeal, tore from the bodies of women what they judged to be indecent clothing.

Converts and critics

Nevertheless, Florence was flourishing under Savonarola's reforms. Artists Botticelli and Michelangelo came to hear Savonarola preach in the Duomo, and they collected and read printed sermons on their own. Donations to San Marco soared. So controversial had Savonarola become, he needed an armed escort to walk the streets. As support increased, so did the envy of his rivals and critics. Monastic orders saw their coffers shrinking as more gifts poured into San Marco. It seemed with every sermon Savonarola gained both more followers and converts, and more political and religious adversaries.

The pope's scrutiny

The pope continued monitoring events in Florence. He was little disturbed by Savonarola's constant harping on moral corruption in the church; he'd heard all that before. And it was all true. He could tolerate anything so long as his supremacy over the church was not threatened. But Savonarola's preaching and his politics might be getting dangerous for the pontiff. It wasn't democracy that bothered him; a weak republic was less a threat than a strong dictatorship, and he had never been a fan of Medici rule. The scheming pope, determined to keep the Holy League alive, deeply resented Florence's refusal to join the league and suspected Savonarola of secretly negotiating with France against the Holy League.

At last Pope Alexander VI decided to craft a letter to Savonarola. It was dated 21 July 1495:

> To our well-beloved son, greetings and the apostolic benediction. We have heard that of all the workers in the Lord's vineyard thou art the most zealous; at which we deeply rejoice, and give thanks to Almighty God. We have likewise heard that thou dost assert that thy predictions proceed not from thee but from God. Therefore we desire, as behooves our pastoral office, to have speech with thee concerning these things; so that, being by these means better informed of God's will, we may be better able to fulfil it. Wheretofore, by thy vow of holy obedience, we enjoin thee to wait on us without delay, and shall welcome thee with loving kindness.

It sounded so congenial, but Savonarola knew better. To disobey the pope's request and refuse to appear before him in Rome would fuel his critics' suspicions. He knew the Borgia's methods; if he obeyed and went to Rome, he could be thrown in prison to rot — or worse. What would happen to his beloved Florence then? Cautiously he wrote back:

> *The Lord having spared this city through me a great effusion of blood and converted it to good and holy laws, there are many enemies both within and without who, having hoped to reduce her to servitude and failed, desire blood and have more than once attempted my life with poison and steel. I cannot suppose that my superior desires the ruin of an entire city, I trust therefore that Your holiness will kindly admit this delay in order that we may bring to perfection this reform begun by the will of the Lord.*

Fuming, the frustrated pope next wrote to the Signoria of Florence, protesting their alliance with France and warning that an alliance with the enemies of Italy would have consequences. The letter ended with a bombshell: Savonarola was to desist from preaching, submit to the authority of the Dominican hierarchy in Lombardy, and was to be reassigned to another priory.

The faction in the Signoria who wanted Savonarola silenced received the papal letter with glee. But they knew that the people would not stand for losing their beloved overseer, so they compromised, consenting only to restricting Savonarola from preaching.

The pope, in a conciliatory response (16 October), repeated his prohibition against Savonarola preaching and expressed the hope that when his health permitted he should come to Rome, to be received in 'a joyful and fatherly spirit'.

Meanwhile, supporters of Savonarola in the Signoria sent their own letter to the pope earnestly appealing for him to withdraw his restriction against the friar's preaching, arguing that Florence needed his preaching for Lent. At last the pope relented, and on 17 February 1496, Savonarola resumed his public preaching in the Duomo. But it would be preaching with papal scrutiny. The pope commissioned a Dominican bishop to examine Savonarola's latest published sermons. The bishop reported:

> *Most Holy Father, this friar says nothing that is not wise and honest; he speaks against simony and the corruption of the priesthood, which in truth is very great; he respects the dogmas and authority of the Church; wherefore I would rather seek to make him my friend if need be by offering him the cardinal's purple.*

In another attempt to bring Savonarola into his camp, Alexander VI offered him the red hat of a cardinal. Incensed, Savonarola replied to the pope's emissary, 'Come to my next sermon, and you will have my reply to Rome.'

Problems with Pisa

With the pope pacified for a while, Savonarola turned his attention toward Florence's foreign affairs. In the wake of the war with France all Italy had turned to rebuilding their economies and replenishing the food stores. The rich farmland around the city of Pisa had always been a source of food for the region, a region that included Florence. That was all changing.

Savonarola had promised to bring Pisa back into the fold of Florence, even claiming at one point to hold Pisa in the hollow of his hand. But Pisa would have none of it, and Savonarola had no means to bring it about. Machiavelli later said, 'Savonarola is a prophet without arms.' In a great act of defiance, the rebellious city built its own alliances, ignoring the wooing of Savonarola or of the Signoria.

Meanwhile, Tuscan neighbours started upping taxes for barge traffic on the Arno River and other trade routes from Florence to the Adriatic Sea. The increased operating costs, coupled with occasional military threats against Florentine trade partners, stifled commerce, and tax revenue fell. Savonarola was learning even a city for God can't have isolationist policies. In a situation resembling early twenty-first century western socialism, bonds were forcibly sold to finance the war with Pisa, but as bankruptcy neared, these bonds quickly dropped to ten per cent of their face value. By 1496 the treasury was empty, and desperate officials dipped into funds that had been set aside to provide dowries for poor brides.

Thus far, it appeared that too many of Savonarola's well-intentioned reforms were a mere cleaning of the outside of the cup. Government corruption and incompetence spread. Savonarola's supporters lashed back at their growing political rivals. The critics of Savonarola were excluded from government councils, and any friar who preached against him was expelled from the city. Then critics in the Signoria summoned Savonarola before a council of ecclesiastics vaguely accusing him of political activities improper in a friar. He replied:

> Now the words of the Lord are fulfilled: 'The sons of my mother have fought against me.' To be concerned with the affairs of this world is no crime in a monk unless he should mix in them without any higher aim, and without seeking to promote the cause of religion.

We hear the weariness in his tone. The man was deeply troubled and discouraged at the relentless infighting engulfing him. Yet this was only the beginning. His enemies' attacks would increase.

9

Bitter fight

Reluctant though Savonarola was to enter the dizzying and dangerous world of politics, he was compelled by the firm belief that he had a divine commission to proclaim God's judgement on the corruption and decadence of Florence. One thing was certain: the status quo was not an option. Leave things as they were, and Florence could not survive the political chaos, the mounting threats from hostile neighbours, and her crushing economic woes, not to mention the wrath of God hanging over the epicentre of decadence in Renaissance Italy.

Nevertheless, the popular spin on Savonarola and his reforms in Florence is summed up by a celebrated travel guru: 'Savonarola cast a spell on the city, but in the end Florentines preferred the Renaissance and the Medicis to a church-sponsored return to the dark ages.' Though this sounds so urbane and enlightened, it only works if we sweep aside many of the facts. For starters, Medici rule was nothing short of thuggery, on a scale with the brutalities of rogue

states in the modern world. Common folks don't matter in
societies bullied by crime bosses like the Medicis, and the
majority had had enough. Restoring Florence to a republic,
what Savonarola was doing, was precisely what the people of
Florence wanted. This fact is lost on historians — and travel
gurus — predisposed against constitutional government
that restrains big government and gives more freedom and
responsibility to the individual. The Signoria and the people
of Florence wanted precisely what Savonarola was preaching
and what he was doing — for a while.

The Bible

It is critical to remember that, in the big picture, what
Savonarola was preaching had its source throughout the
pages of the Bible, and not merely back in the clean pages
of the Old Testament. The apostle Paul wanted to wake his
listeners from sleep with these words:

> *The night is far gone; the day is at hand. So then let us cast
> off the works of darkness and put on the armour of light.
> Let us walk properly as in the daytime, not in orgies and
> drunkenness, not in sexual immorality and sensuality, not in
> quarrelling and jealousy. But put on the Lord Jesus Christ,
> and make no provision for the flesh, to gratify its desires
> (Romans 13:12-14).*

The Renaissance was a rebirth of all things Greek and
Roman, and in Florence the orgies and drunkenness, the
sexual immorality, and certainly the quarrelling and political
infighting had been reborn in spades, just as it was in

Rome in Paul's day. Savonarola understood that if Florence
persisted in her free fall into the abyss and darkness of her
sins, she would be destroyed. Evidence of that destruction
already lay all about the city.

'Evil man is a servant to his sins and is not free,' Savonarola
declared from his pulpit in the Duomo. His first concern
was the salvation of the souls of the people in Florence, but
he knew that their sin and corruption enslaved them, in this
life and in the one to come. In this life, their wickedness
precluded them from being good citizens and from
virtuously serving their neighbours in their city. He knew,
long before Alexis de Tocqueville famously observed in his
Democracy in America, that Florence could never be great
until it was good.

A daily reader of his Bible, Savonarola knew what caused
the ruin even of the best of the kings of Israel and Judah.
Because they did not utterly tear down the high places
and idols, they were enslaved by the false worship around
them, and eventually scattered over the face of the earth, a
destitute people without a city. His reading of John's vision
in Revelation, moreover, led him to conclude that the time
had come; Christ's return in judgement was imminent.

Bonfires

In early 1496 Florentines made ready for their winter
carnival, a festival roughly equivalent to the average Friday
and Saturday night on university campuses today. But they
did their sinning with style in Florence. There were masks

and gaudy costumes, lewd entertainments, drinking and dancing in the streets, and huge bonfires that blazed late into the night.

Wild as the official festivities were, things often spun out of control into violence. Obscene behaviour and debauchery gave way to gang fights, barricades, property damage, robbery, rape, knifings and other thuggery.

To counter the sordidness, Savonarola mobilized his 'boys of San Marco', who put up crosses and marched around with crucifixes. Wearing white smocks to symbolize purity, they shouted, 'Hurray for Christ the King.' They collected alms and zealously gathered pornographic pictures and books, gambling devices, and vain clothing. On 16 February 1496 they threw all these into a pile and ignited the first of many 'Bonfires of the Vanities'.

More trouble

In June, word of another attempted French invasion circulated, and papal pressure mounted to force Florence into the Holy League. Still the Signoria refused. Meanwhile, other Italian city-states mobilized and hired mercenaries — but then the threat collapsed. The mercenaries had been paid in advance and were keeping their money. Not about to waste the hired muscle, the League blockaded Florence. Natural disaster compounded Florence's economic woes; heavy rains fell almost daily, ruining many crops in Tuscany. Florence's poverty seemed to be coming upon her.

Meanwhile, Savonarola ramped up his exposé of papal corruption. 'One thousand, ten thousand, fourteen thousand harlots are few for Rome, for there both men and women are made harlots.' Supporters of Savonarola published pamphlets hailing him as a prophet and a saint; while Savonarola's enemies, like today's bloggers, worked the printing presses overtime accusing him of heresy. News spread far and wide; even the sultan of Turkey followed the rhetoric.

Determined to silence Savonarola, the pope attempted a reorganization of Dominican monasteries into a new order under his control, and then issued a transfer order for Savonarola that would put him out to pasture in a backwater priory. 'This union is impossible, unreasonable, and hurtful,' Savonarola wrote. 'The brethren of San Marco cannot be bound to it, inasmuch as superiors may not issue commands contrary to the rules of the order, nor contrary to the law of charity or the welfare of our souls.' The pope was enraged; Savonarola publicly defied him — and had the support of the majority in Florence. Next Savonarola attacked the pope from the pulpit, 'The pope may not give any command opposed to charity or the Gospel.' If the pope were to do so, Savonarola would say to him, 'Now thou art no pastor, thou art not the Church of Rome, thou art in error.'

Sounding like Samuel Rutherford in *Lex Rex* (1644), Savonarola knew the extent of his loyalties, but he was obviously learning a measure of tact. 'Whenever it be clearly seen that the commands of superiors are contrary to God's commandments, and especially when contrary to the precepts of charity, no one is in such case bound to obedience.' He remained resolute. 'I would obey no living man that commanded me to depart [Florence], because in obeying him I should disobey the commands of the Lord.'

The pope took no immediate action, but rumours of excommunication seeped out of Rome.

Craving the cross

By early 1497, once prosperous Florence was gripped with starvation. Savonarola placed the blame squarely on corruption in the church. 'Riches are what have ruined her. The church would be better off without riches, because there would be more union with God. Therefore I tell my monks, cling to poverty, for when riches come in, death enters the house.' In his next breath he resumed his attack on the clergy:

> The earth is full of blood and they do not care; nay, they murder souls by their bad examples. They have departed from God and their cult is to spend the whole night with whores and the day gossipping in the sacristies. Once you blushed for your sins, but not now. O whore of a church, you have shown your foulness to the whole world and your stench rises to heaven.

How much could the Roman pontiff endure? Savonarola was about to find out, and his blood was up. In words anticipatory of Luther's, he declared:

*I tell you that we must burst this sepulchre. Christ wants
to resuscitate his Church in spirit, we must all pray for this
renovation. Write to France, to Germany, write everywhere
and say, 'This friar bids you to go to the Lord and pray, for his
return.' God will call me, then I will send forth a great voice
which will be heard in all Christendom, and it will make the
body of the church tremble.*

Clearly Savonarola knew the blast radius of his words
extended to Rome, and clearly he too had heard papal threats
of excommunication: 'Bring it on, the excommunication,
bring it in on a spear. I know that there are those in Rome
who are toiling against me night and day, but O Lord, this
is what I desire. I crave only your cross, make me to be
persecuted. I ask you this grace; that you do not let me die
in my bed.'

It is difficult to silence a man who speaks this way. Not only
Florentines, but people from all over northern Italy packed
into the Duomo to hear Savonarola declare what was true
about the Church. Savonarola organized prayer assemblies,
and fasting was so common that butchers petitioned for
rebates on their taxes.

As the Lenten season approached, and another winter
carnival with it, Savonarola renewed his denunciations of
vanities. He called for all the families of Florence, along
with the San Marco boys, to gather all immoral pictures,
love songs, carnival masks and costumes, false hair, fancy
dresses, playing cards, dice, facepaint and pornographic
books. On the final night of the carnival, Savonarola's

supporters sang hymns and marched in solemn procession behind four children carrying a figure of the Infant Jesus carved by Donatello. At the *Plaza della Signoria* they threw their vanities into a massive pile, including manuscripts of Plato and Aristotle and nude paintings by Botticelli. As the flames rose high into the air, the bells of the old palace rang in celebration.

Pressure mounting

But the famine raged on, people literally dropping dead from starvation. Scrambling desperately to find food, some were trampled in the streets. A growing faction tried to fix the blame on Savonarola, and while preaching on Ascension Day, rioters interrupted his sermon and tried to kidnap him. His followers intervened.

In April, Piero de Medici made an attempt to grab power. The heavily indebted prince was backed by 1,000 unemployed Florentines. Drenching rain pummelled the city and dampened further support of the failed prince. In August, Piero's supporters tried to restore the prince with an internal coup. When the plot was discovered, Savonarola seized the leaders, and tried and convicted them without appeal. Within hours they were beheaded. Hostile crowds demonstrated before San Marco and hurled rocks in the streets.

Plague, starvation, and now injustice. A tarnished Savonarola attempted to explain the big picture:

Death is the solemn moment of your life; it is then that the devil delivers his supreme battle. It is as if he played chess with man all his days, waiting for the approach of death to checkmate him. To win that move is to win the battle of life. O my brothers, we live in the world only to learn how to die.

The crowds dispersed, but they would be back.

Excommunication

The tide was turning for Savonarola. As his followers diminished, Rome made her move. On 16 June 1497, the pope excommunicated Savonarola and forbade him from preaching. Unable to speak to the people of Florence, his popularity plummeted like Galileo's weights from the tower of Pisa. The new social order began to disintegrate. Despite Savonarola's preaching, many in his flock had had no change of their sinful nature. Like dogs to their vomit, many Florentines eagerly returned to their taverns, brothels and gambling halls. Vice engulfed public virtue almost overnight.

As if to bring on the wrath of the pope, Savonarola sang the liturgy on Christmas Day at San Marco, gave the Eucharist to his friars, and led a solemn procession around the square. Howling the excommunicated friar's defiance of the pope, Florence issued printed demands that Savonarola be punished. But the pope was more a diplomat than a cleric, and was about to reveal his temporal priorities.

As rumours of yet another French invasion blew through the snowy passes of the Alps, the shrewd pope had another card up his sleeve. He offered to lift Savonarola's excommunication if Florence would join the Holy League. On 11 February 1498 Savonarola upped the stakes by preaching against the pope at San Marco. In the sermon he denounced the excommunication as unjust and invalid, and charged with heresy any man who upheld its validity. With a bold stroke, he issued a counter-excommunication:

> *Therefore, on him that gives commands opposed to charity let there be a curse. Were such a command pronounced by an angel, even by the Virgin Mary herself and all the saints (which is certainly impossible), let there be curses. And if any pope hath ever spoken to the contrary, let him be declared excommunicated.*

Calculated to provoke, after launching this salvo, Savonarola next dropped hints about performing a miracle. 'As yet I have not been constrained to a miracle, but in his own time, the Lord will extend his hand.'

Yanking off his boots, Savonarola here exposes his feet of clay. As with so many who enter the political arena, he may have discovered that the lions are circling, and they're vicious and hungry. In a classic example of a man hoisting himself on his own petard, Savonarola's words put everyone on watch to see if he could deliver on the miracle — especially watchful were his critics. The noose was tightening, but it was a noose Savonarola had helped to tie.

10

Ordeal by fire

In further defiance of the pope, on Fat (Shrove) Tuesday 1498, Savonarola celebrated the mass on the cobblestoned plaza before San Marco, administering the sacrament to a large and needy crowd. 'O Lord, if my deeds be not sincere,' he prayed, 'if my words be not inspired by Thee, strike me dead this instant.' That afternoon his followers staged a second 'Bonfire of the Vanities', but many Florentines added garbage and dead animals instead of their pornography and gambling devices; a black layer of foul-smelling smoke filled the plaza.

By now the opposition party had won a large majority in the Signoria, but Savonarola and his followers persisted. Machiavelli, after hearing Savonarola preach in March, wrote:

> Our friar, being in his own house, you should have heard with what boldness he began his sermons and with what recklessness he followed them up. You would have been no

little amazed, for being profoundly unsure of himself, yet
believing that the new Signoria wouldn't harm him, and
realizing that many citizens would be buried under his ruin,
he began with great terrors, with reasons most compelling to
those who did not dispute them, proving his own followers
to be the salt of the earth and his enemies scoundrels, and
touching every point which could weaken his opponents.

Savonarola was not backing down. After hearing another sermon, Machiavelli said, somewhat ironically for a pragmatist, 'Savonarola is a time-serving and self-seeking demagogue, veering with every shift of the political wind.' Lost on the author of *The Prince* was Savonarola's passion — the eternal salvation of souls. Curiously, Machiavelli gained political office in the very republic Savonarola helped established, but when the Medicis regained power in 1512, they predictably banished Machiavelli from public life.

While Savonarola's reforms were hitting bottom in Italian politics, he was gaining support from France and Germany. The pope had to act. Murdering the rogue friar was the thing to do but would be too obvious. He decided to flex his ecclesiastical muscle: he told the Signoria to silence Savonarola's preaching or he would place Florence under interdict, thereby damning everyone in the city to hell.

More concerned with the effect interdict might have on trade than the threat of damnation, and perhaps still partially attuned to Savonarola's message, the Signoria decided to let him continue preaching, thus creating a temporary reprieve for the prior of San Marco.

Rome cranked up the rhetoric. In time the Florentine ambassador to Rome wrote that feelings against Savonarola had become so harsh that no Florentine was safe in Rome. Another rumour floated north that if the pope inflicted the interdict, it would also include jailing all Florentine merchants.

Still the Signoria hesitated. Finally, Florentine merchants abroad complained about threats to their commercial health. At last the Signoria yielded. On 17 March 1498, Savonarola was ordered to desist from preaching. For the moment, after predicting great calamity on Florence, he obeyed.

Intercepted

Abandoned by the pope, and at war with the Signoria, Savonarola wrote to the sovereigns of France, Spain, Germany and Hungary asking them to organize a general council for the reform of the Church.

> *The moment of vengeance has arrived. The Lord commands me to reveal new secrets, and make manifest to the world the peril by which the bark of St Peter is threatened, owing to your long neglect. The Church is all teeming with abomination, from the crown of her head to the soles of her feet; yet not only do ye apply no remedy, but ye do homage to the cause of the woes by which she is polluted. Wherefore the Lord is greatly angered, and hath long left the Church without a shepherd.*

The gloves were off now. If his ministry and his life were to be ended by the pope, he wanted to make something crystal clear to everyone — before his voice was silenced: 'For I hereby testify that this Alexander is no pope, nor can he be held as one; inasmuch as leaving aside the mortal sin of simony, by which he hath purchased the papal chair, and daily sells the benefices of the Church to the highest bidder, and likewise putting aside his other manifest vices, I declare that he is no Christian, and believes in no God.'

If the pope read this, it would seal Savonarola's doom. And then a papal agent from Milan intercepted the letter and delivered it to the pope. Meanwhile, Savonarola had sent off another letter addressed to the pope. The pope read it first:

> I have always thought it the duty of a good Christian to defend the faith and correct morals, but in this labour I have encountered only trials and tribulations. Not one man would aid me. I had hoped in your holiness, but you have preferred to join my enemies and give fierce wolves leave to torment me cruelly. No heed has been paid to the reasons I gave, not to excuse my error, but to prove the truth of my doctrine, my innocence and my obedience to the church.

Ever-forthright Savonarola proceeded to abandon all confidence in the pope, alluding to what the apostle Paul wrote concerning sovereign election, 'God chose what is weak in the world to shame the strong' (1 Corinthians 1:27b):

> I can no longer hope in your holiness. I must turn to him who elects the weak of this world to confound the strong lions of

the wicked. He will aid me to sustain and prove against the whole world the sanctity of this work for which I suffer so much. He will inflict the just penalty on those who persecute me and attempt to prevent it. For myself, I seek no earthly glory but wait death with eagerness. I implore your holiness to delay no longer.

The pope saw Savonarola's words as an open threat to his person and as a man itching for martyrdom. And then his aides handed him the intercepted letter of Savonarola's sent to the pope's enemies. In his rage, he may have turned as red as his pontifical vestments.

Ordeal by fire

What occurred next, incredible as it sounds to us, helps the modern reader of history to better understand the credulous world in which Savonarola lived. On 25 March 1498 a Franciscan friar took Savonarola to task for declaring himself a prophet and claiming to have miraculous power. In a dramatic flourish, the rival friar challenged Savonarola to an ordeal by fire.

Ordeal by fire had a long history, dating back to the fiery furnace in the book of Daniel, though the important differences between the Old Covenant and the New were lost on nearly everyone in Savonarola's day.

Ordeal by fire was not a first for Florence. According to medieval legend, in the twelfth century a monk had cleared himself of slanderous charges by walking over red-hot ploughshares — without getting burned. Ordeal by fire was believed to sift out, once and for all, which man had the favour of God. Even in enlightened Florence, the majority still believed such a trial would prove which man was on God's side. For the sceptic, ordeal by fire made a good show.

Privately, the Franciscan friar confessed that he would burn, but he was fine with that because he was pretty sure his Dominican rival would burn too.

But Savonarola was urged to refuse the challenge, his friend and supporter Fra Domenico insisting on taking his prior's place. When the ordeal by fire was announced in a sermon, women cried out, 'I too! I too!' Not to be outdone, hundreds of men volunteered to take Domenico's place.

Peeved that Savonarola himself would not perish, the Signoria agreed to the spectacle in the hope of discrediting him. They had conspired behind closed doors that when Domenico perished, they would send Savonarola into exile within three hours.

Preparing the *Piazza de Signoria* for the ordeal by fire, workers laboured feverishly. As if blood sports from the ancient Roman Coliseum had been reinstated, Italians talked of little else. Bets were placed. Pilgrims flocked to Florence. Like Black Friday at Wal-Mart, for days people camped in the plaza in the hope of getting the best seats. Either they would see a miracle — or the spectacular deaths of two human beings. It was a toss-up which would be more impressive to the gathered mob.

Florentines constructed high window seating and fitted their rooftops for viewing the spectacle — vantage points available for a price. Meanwhile, henchmen prepared the path the two friars would have to navigate for the ordeal. They constructed a corridor of wood covered with pitch, oil, resin and gunpowder; the passage was only two feet wide but sixty feet long. When ignited it would be a flaming inferno to stir Dante in his grave. No living thing could survive the first step into the incinerating labyrinth — unless God supernaturally intervened.

The Signoria permitted only men to watch the spectacle to 'avoid an explosion of passion from the weaker sex'. Nevertheless, there was no shortage of women and children infiltrating the crowd. Anticipating a riot, the Signoria placed two companies of armed men in reserve.

Divine intervention

7 April 1498; the day had arrived. The crowds held back by 300 Florentine guards armed with pikes, 200 grey-clad Franciscans with covered heads and hands clasped in prayer paraded into the plaza. They took up positions in front of the eastern end of the Loggia, the covered veranda in front of the old palace.

From the opposite side of the plaza entered 250 black-hooded Dominicans followed by a huge crowd of men, women and children holding candles. For days they had fasted, and they had passed the night in a solemn prayer vigil. Domenico wore a red cape and carried the consecrated host, a loaf of bread representing Christ's body. Behind him walked Savonarola dressed in white and holding a crucifix. They positioned themselves on the opposite end of the Loggia.

With ranks formed, Savonarola preached that his words and manner needed no miraculous confirmation and that he had never sought to justify himself with miracles. He declared that, as on Mount Carmel, miracles could only be expected in answer to earnest prayer. Thinking he was hedging his bets, many in the crowd booed over his words.

The hour had come. It was time to ignite the inferno. But then the Franciscans lodged a complaint; they protested that Domenico's red cape might be mystically empowered by Savonarola; they feared it just might be magically fire retardant. The Dominicans countered the protest, and the bickering began.

Anxious for the contest to begin, the bloodthirsty crowd shouted over the friars. Finally Domenico agreed to take off the cape. But the Franciscans then demanded that he replace his other garments. Weary of it all, Domenico agreed. When he came back from the changing room in the palace, they ordered him to keep clear of Savonarola. For all their dislike of the man, they certainly had an elevated view of his powers. Next they surrounded Domenico, insisting that he give up the crucifix and the host. Domenico handed over the crucifix but refused to let go of the host. The crowds were growing restless; they had not gathered to watch a petty brawl between monastic orders.

What followed was a scholars' debate about whether it would be blasphemy for the host, the body of Christ, to be taken into the fire. If Domenico succumbed in the flames, the sacred bread might perish with him. Savonarola entered the debate, arguing that even if Domenico be burned to a crisp, the body of Christ could never be consumed. Flustered, the Franciscans ran in and out of the palace, consulting with the Signoria, raising objections and stalling the ordeal. Anxious for the flaming spectacle, the crowds grew more restless.

All the while, clouds had been forming over the city. Suddenly the heavens opened and rain fell in torrents. Cheated out of the ordeal, the crowd surged forward, pushing against the guards, threatening to burn them all. Still the friars danced on the head of a pin in debate. Meanwhile, inside the palace the Franciscan champion, experiencing a failure of nerve, begged the Signoria to save him from the ordeal by any means possible.

It had rained on their parade, and by dinner time the soaked and hungry crowd had had enough. They threw rocks and started fist fights. The situation was nearly out of control. The guards moved from restraint to force; blood was spilt. The Signoria was on the verge of losing control of the city.

From the balcony of the old palace a city official appeared, screaming over the chaos that the event was over. He then dashed back in to avoid the shower of stones. The Signoria may have hoped to discredit both orders and strengthen their own hand; but the crowd, cheated of blood, attacked the guards. The reserves stormed in, swords bared and pikes levelled, driving back the mob and chasing them through the streets.

With the soldiers now occupied elsewhere, the opposition party made their move; they tried to grab Savonarola and take him into custody, but a phalanx of black friars surrounded him and repulsed their scheme.

Amidst jeers, and showers of stones, rotten fruit and vegetables, his supporters surrounded Savonarola and pushed their way back to San Marco. A tense hour of fending off the mob elapsed before they finally entered the protective walls of the convent and barred the doors.

Papal response

Meanwhile, back in Rome the pope anxiously awaited news from Florence. Officially he had been forced to disapprove of the ordeal by fire; nevertheless, he saw it as an easy way to be rid of Savonarola. The dust had not settled, and the pope officially hailed the Franciscans in extravagant terms, declaring that they could not have done anything more agreeable to him.

But the people of Florence had been cheated out of a good show, and they cast about for someone to blame. Aided by the rhetoric of Savonarola's critics, many jumped ship and made their choice: Savonarola was no longer the solution to their problems; he was the cause of them. The pope was elated. Now he would have his revenge on the man who had declared him no Christian.

11

Arrest and trial

Savonarola's influence over the majority of Florence was over. Cheated out of a miracle or a spectacle, they grumbled in the streets, 'If only Savonarola had stood the ordeal by fire,' and, 'He claimed to be God's prophet,' and 'Why did he not work a miracle?'

As workers cleaned up the plaza, the unrest mounted. Savonarola had not entered the fire. For many, that settled the matter: he was a fraud. They would have felt more kindly toward him if he had died in the flames.

The next day was Palm Sunday, and a friar loyal to Savonarola was to preach in the Duomo. On the way, he was accosted by men, members of the wealthy Compagnacci, who began shoving him and spitting in his face. Next he was forced to pass through a throng of boys pelting the faithful with rocks and hurling obscenities at them. When he finally ducked into the cathedral, he found the benches packed with anxious congregants.

As he prepared to begin the service, men embedded in the congregation drew their swords and fell on the friar and any who stood with him. Beating with the flats of their swords, they broke up the service, with churchgoers fleeing for their lives from the cathedral.

Clearing the doors, they were met with a shower of rocks thrown by a gang of boys. Worse yet, surging toward the cathedral from the *Piazza del Signoria* was another mob packing clubs, homemade spears, even small cannons, and shouting, 'On to San Marco!' The mob swirled around the Duomo then turned northeast toward San Marco and Savonarola. Along the way, the homes of many followers of the prior were pelted with stones and arrows. More than a few occupants were killed, and houses were ransacked, survivors scattering in terror.

Riot at San Marco

The friars at San Marco heard the rumbling of the approaching mob. Aware of the mounting tensions and likelihood of violence, a friar named Silvestro had orchestrated the arming of the monastery with guns, swords, crossbows and halberds (hatchets). Some of the friars had been soldiers before taking their vows; they knew what to do with weapons, and they understood what would happen if they didn't use them.

'*Viva Cristo*,' they shouted, barring the doors and slamming the heavy shutters over the windows. Black-robed archers took up their positions and prepared to face the mob swelling into the plaza. Above them the bells of the tower rang for help, while in the plaza below bloodied and bruised citizens fleeing before the mob tried to escape the rampage.

Unaware of his friars' weapons cache, Savonarola looked on in horror. Not wanting blood on his hands, he tried to stop the brothers from resorting to arms, but they were desperate for their lives. 'This storm is for me,' cried Savonarola, striding purposefully toward the front gate, rocks clattering against its timbers. Fearing for their prior's life, they grabbed him and led him to the altar of the church, he begging them to lay down their weapons.

Fearful of being trapped inside the priory, many of the refugees chose to take their chances outside the walls. In panic, many ran out of side doors, slid out of windows, or crawled through a tunnel that led underground to the old student college.

Siege

The attackers next took control of the plaza before San Marco and the streets surrounding it. Like a scene from Victor Hugo's *Les Miserables*, angry rioters threw up barricades and waved banners in the air. Mounted on horseback, the ringleaders formed companies and led a charge on the priory. Next they stacked bundles of wood and barrels of pitch against the gates, but the friars cut down the attackers with their arrows. Not expecting armed resistance from Dominican friars, the attackers fell back, leaving their dead and wounded bleeding on the cobblestones.

Little is known of Savonarola's movements at this point. Fearing for his doomed friars, he may have called for greater resistance to avoid a massacre. After all, he had taught that enemies are often God's instruments of judgement on his enemies. The defence stiffened.

The stalwart friars held off yet another assault, until finally the opposition sent a legation under a flag of truce demanding their surrender. Determined to protect their prior, they refused. The besiegers then positioned catapults, cannons and siege ladders.

The attackers were determined. In their next assault they succeeded in setting the wooden gates ablaze. When the flames died down, the mob breached the walls. What followed was several hours of bitter fighting surging through the cloisters and galleries of the priory. 'Save thy people, Lord!' cried the friars, but the attackers were too many.

Amidst cannon fire and the clashing of steel, Savonarola ascended the pulpit and did what he did best: he preached. Women and children, shaking with fear, and bloodied friars listened to his anguished words:

> What I have said I have heard from God, and he is my witness in heaven that I do not tell lies. I did not know that the city would turn against me so soon, but the Lord's will be done. My last word is this: 'Faith, patience, and prayer are your arms.' I leave you with anguish and sorrow, to place myself in the hands of our enemies. I do not know if they will take my life, but I am certain that if I should die I can help you more from heaven than I have been able in life. Have courage, embrace the cross, and you will find the port of salvation.

In the darkness, the smoke and the debris, he fell to his knees and prayed. About midnight, the mob issued a final ultimatum, threatening complete annihilation if the friars did not immediately capitulate.

Four leaders entered the priory to declare their terms. San Marco would be spared and armed guards posted to prevent further plundering and damage. In exchange Savonarola and his two top aides, Fra Domenico and Fra Silvestro, would give themselves up. Savonarola told the legates that he feared the friars would be torn to pieces if they stepped outside. The mob promised an armed escort.

Moments later, Savonarola and Domenico, their hands cinched tightly behind their backs, were led through the mob, their escorts holding back the people with their halberds. The street was lined with spitting and jeering protestors to their jail cells at the Palazzo Vecchio. One man broke through the guards. 'He has his prophecy up his backside,' he yelled, kicking Savonarola. Another shoved a torch in the prior's face and yelled, 'Here is the true light.'

In the early morning hours, the two friars were separated; Savonarola was led up the bell tower and clamped in leg irons. It was only the beginning of the ordeal.

Torture

Hours after Savonarola's arrival, the Signoria sent a letter to the pope giving their account of the siege and the arrest of the man who was such a thorn in the side of the pontiff. They ended the letter with a description of their plans to elicit true confession from the prisoners by all means — including torture. The pope quickly agreed, but wanted the trial held in an ecclesiastical court in Rome. The Signoria refused, and the pope was forced to settle with having a few of his delegates assist the eight men assigned to perform the inquisition. Before commencing the trial, all agreed that Savonarola must die. To let him live would keep his movement alive and continue damaging Florence's credibility in Italy and abroad.

While the correspondence was carried to and from Rome, the prosecutors of Savonarola displayed the weapons used to defend San Marco. Mocking the prior, they taunted him on account of the arms, asking him if this is how caring, peaceful and loving friars fulfilled their vows.

With the formalities complete, the court got down to work. They decided to break Savonarola's will by accusing him of religious posturing, heavy-handedness in Florentine politics, illegal involvement with enemies of Florence and Italy, his domination of the Signoria, obtaining political secrets from men in the confessional booth, and entering into alliance with the enemies of Italy.

To secure his confession of these alleged crimes against Florence and the Signoria, Savonarola was placed on the rack and stretched.

Few men can withstand sustained torture without breaking under the unrelenting agony — though Hollywood tells another tale. The justice of the cause notwithstanding, men can only rarely bear up under prolonged, purposefully inflicted suffering. American prisoners of war in North

Vietnam's infamous Hanoi Hilton broke after courageous stands against their torturers. Precise and intentional infliction of pain is a tremendous motivator. Savonarola was a man, and his tormentors knew it.

Early in the sadistic procedure, a procedure that actually ripped bone sockets apart, Savonarola keenly felt the agony and babbled and screamed incoherent answers. Given a few minutes to recover, he immediately reaffirmed his teachings. After more rounds of stretching, tearing and popping, the process proved too much for one of the inquisitors who begged to be dismissed from his duty. Savonarola didn't have that option. Again they set the machinery of torture in motion, but with the same conclusion.

Frustrated at not getting the right answers and with the pope in Rome snapping at their heels to get the job done, the henchmen redoubled their efforts. Over the next ten days and after fourteen bouts of racking torture the inquisitors managed to wring out of Savonarola, now delirious with suffering, the following confession:

> As for my intention and the purpose for which I was working, I reply that it was for my glory and to have reputation and credit. For this purpose I sought to maintain myself in good esteem in the city of Florence, which seemed to me to be an apt instrument to increase this glory and gain credit abroad as well, particularly when I saw that I was believed. To further this purpose I preached things that would convince Christians of the abominations that were practised in Rome. If the council which I expected had been summoned, I hoped to depose many prelates and also the pope. I would have

tried to be present and to preach in Rome to do such things
as would have brought me glory.

Crafting the words for him, the inquisition had generously not broken Savonarola's right arm so he could sign it.

When the confession was published, the friars at San Marco were thrown into consternation. 'My heart was pained to see such an edifice crumble,' one of them wrote. Terrified of the torture that Savonarola had endured, and fearing the same might fall on them, they were persuaded to write an official confession:

> *Not only us but men of much greater intelligence were deceived by the astuteness of Fra Girolamo. The penetration of his doctrine, the rectitude of his life, the sanctity of his habits, his simulated devotion, the benefit he obtained by ridding the town of usury, bad customs, and vice of every kind, and the many events which, surpassing all human effort and imagination, confirmed his prophecies, were such that if he had not retracted and said that his word did not come from God, we could never have denied him our faith.*

Obviously written under duress, they spent many more words praising Savonarola than denouncing their loyalty to him. When it was published, the confession was met with scepticism by the public, and a second trial was arranged. After three days the proceedings were dropped. The word of the examiners would have to be enough.

But there was still Savonarola's closest allies, Silvestro and Domenico, to deal with. They were shown the confession and the rack. Fearful that he would be unable to endure such torment, Silvestro answered his examiners so quickly that his confession was deemed useless by the court. Terrified for his life, he pleaded for an appeal.

Domenico, on the other hand, broke the mould. Resolute under the most excruciating agonies, he resisted so long without breaking that he almost succumbed without a word. When at last he could endure no more, he gave an equivocating denouncement of Savonarola. Smitten with remorse, and in a final act of defiance against his tormentors, he asked to be burned alive without being hanged till dead first.

Charged with schism and heresy, with spreading confessional secrets, with false visions and prophecies, and with causing disorder in the state, with unanimous consent of the state and church, Savonarola and his followers were condemned to death. Always looking for the right political effect, the pope absolved them of their sins, but gave them no clemency.

'It is enough Lord', cried Savonarola, 'now take my soul.'

12

The flames

Girolamo Savonarola was alone. Had he not saved the supporters of the Medicis when Piero had fled? Had he not saved the city from the ravages of Charles VIII and his French army? Had he not brought democracy to corrupt Florence? Except for a few — very few — his supporters had deserted him.

Scribbling feverishly with his pen, the forty-six-year-old prior waged a war with his inner man in self-deprecating soliloquy. 'How long will you be a weakling? How long before you learn how to fight? You have been so often in battle, and are half now in the shadow of death, and you have not learned yet how to fight. Take courage, coward.'

Why had he not stood fast under the agonies of torture? He had endured self-inflicted pain for two decades. Why when his tormenters inflicted pain on his body had he recanted what he had preached and done, his life's work, the work God himself had told him to do? He was haunted by his own frailties in the darkness of his cell.

The gift of faith

Then his tormented mind began to recollect Scripture, his soul finding comfort in the words of the God who had commissioned him. Not from a vision or prophecy, but from the Bible: the Psalms, the Law, the Gospels, the Epistles — all commingling in his biblically informed imagination:

> Sinner that I am, where shall I turn now? To the Lord whose mercy is infinite. No one can glory in himself; all the saints say, not of us but of the Lord is glory. They were not saved by their merit, nor by their work, but by the goodness and grace of God, that nobody may glory in himself.

And once he began, the words of Holy Scripture came like a flood, but it was no engulfing torrent; it was a healing balm that washed over him. 'If armies are arrayed against me, my heart will know no more fear, because you are my refuge and will lead me to my goal.'

As the evil hour approached, his meditations centred more precisely on the free mercy of God, and he posed the all-important question to himself: 'Do you have faith? Yes I have it. Good: this is a great grace of God, for faith comes of his gift, not of your works, that no one may glory in them.' As martyrdom drew near, it was as if Savonarola's theology took on a new clarity, less influenced by the medieval mingle-mangle of faith and works, more like Luther's who would follow him. He seemed now to see with crystal clarity that even faith was a gift of the unmerited mercy of God.

Grace to endure

Only days before this, city officials erected a gibbet in the shape of a cross with a platform leading back to the Palazzo de Vecchio. Three nooses of hemp drifted ominously in a light breeze. Below the platform they had stacked bundles of dry sticks, at the ready to light a great conflagration.

Their last night on earth, Savonarola and his faithful fellow-sufferers were permitted time together. To his devoted servant, Fra Domenico, Savonarola encouraged him in the grace of God: 'I know that you have asked to be burned alive, but that is not right. Do we know our own strength? Do you know how we will meet the death to which we are doomed? That depends, not on us, but on the grace which the Lord will allow us.' Next Savonarola urged faithful Fra Silvestro to follow Christ's example in suffering: 'I know that you wish to defend your innocence before the people. I command you to abandon such a thought and to follow the example of Jesus Christ, who not even on the cross would speak of his innocence.'

Time was short, and the condemned men were returned to their cells where a priest waited to hear their final confession. Savonarola concluded his confession with these words: 'Pray God for me, that he may give me strength at my last end and that the enemy may have no power over me.' At peace, he then fell asleep, his head cradled on the lap of his confessor.

Defrocked

The ritual of defrocking and degrading originated in the ancient Roman army. Meant to publicly humiliate a man, the Church augmented it into an elaborate object lesson. The two-hour ritual began at 8.00 in the morning of 23 May. Savonarola, Domenico and Silvestro were brought out of the *Palazzo de Vecchio* and were paraded before a jeering crowd, persuaded to attend by the Signoria laying on ample free food and wine.

Jutting into the *Piazza del Signoria*, city officials had custom-built for the occasion an elevated wooden platform. Onto this Savonarola and his companions were led before the papal envoy, the head of the Dominican order, and representatives of the Signoria. There they stood in their Dominican habits with the implements of their office in their hands. An erstwhile follower of Savonarola had been chosen to be master of ceremonies before officials of church and state. He did his honours methodically and with relish.

Next the turncoat bishop gave out a public reading of the court's findings, convicting them of heresy, schism, and denying the authority of the pope. With each condemnation they were stripped of portions of their robe, or the chalice or communion plate was torn from their hands. After that, like the White Witch with Aslan, they were ceremonially shaven — head, face, even the hair on their hands — thereby removing their tonsure and the holy oil with which they had been ordained.

Meanwhile, the crowd cursed and struggled to break through the guards. Now bald, barefooted, and wearing only a thin under-robe, their degradation was complete, and the three condemned men were roughly escorted before the civil authorities. At this point in the proceedings, there occurred a sudden turn of events. At the eleventh hour, the pope offered them a plenary indulgence, whereby they would be whisked past purgatory and straight to heaven. Perhaps he hoped to appear merciful and thereby gain support from his critics.

The time was near. A priest, dressed in the bold colours of his rank, asked Savonarola: 'In what spirit do you bear this?' Savonarola answered: 'The Lord has suffered much for me.'

Boys enjoying the festivities of the event had crawled under the platform and poked sharp sticks through the cracks. Savonarola and his companions tried their best to avoid these with their bare feet as they were led to the scaffold — and the three nooses.

'Jesus, Jesus, Jesus,' Silvestro repeated as they took their last steps. Meanwhile Domenico, seemingly grateful for a martyr's death, recited the *Te Deum*: 'We praise thee, O God: we acknowledge thee to be the Lord.'

At last they halted at the base of the twenty-three-foot-high scaffold. Gazing upward, they began climbing the steps, the crowd booing in frustration at the three men's composure. Suddenly a clump of men bearing lit torches broke through the guards. Apparently they wanted to see the condemned men burn alive. As they prepared to hurl their torches at the pile of dry sticks, the guards grabbed them, threw them to the ground, and stamped out their torches.

Silvestro was to be the first to go. The executioner placed the noose over his bald head and cinched it tight, stepped back and shoved the man off the scaffold. Silvestro lurched forward, but the noose was stiff and failed to tighten. Kicking and jerking, the condemned man flailed at the slowly constricting knot. Elated, the mob cheered and shouted, then fell silent as Silvestro's body became limp. Next they placed the noose around Domenico's neck. At the bottom of his fall, his neck mercifully broke with a loud snap. He died instantly.

At last, the execution turned to the last man. Roughly, he grabbed Savonarola's arm and shoved him toward the noose. Oddly, Savonarola made a final request. Knowing his thin robe would fly up as his body fell, he asked for a cord to tie his tunic at his ankles. The hooded executioner sneered and yanked the noose over Savonarola's head.

Savonarola gazed out on the upturned faces of the crowd. In all likelihood, he recognized those faces, real people who had turned those same faces upward to him in the pulpit of the Duomo as he had warned them of the wrath to come and urged them to repent and turn to Jesus for the forgiveness of their many trespasses. He may have detected the same longing for words of truth and deliverance that he had seen in many of those faces in the past. But many more mocked him, and jeered him with their words and looks. He hesitated. Ought he to speak to them, one last time?

'Now prophet,' one man taunted from the crowd. 'Show thy power and work a miracle.' Others guffawed and joined in the railing. Savonarola did not speak. Instead he may have been reciting to himself from his vast repository of Scripture, 'As a sheep before his shearers is dumb, so he opened not his mouth.' But he said nothing.

'I separate thee,' pronounced the turncoat bishop, 'from the church militant and triumphant!'

Unable to keep silent, Savonarola replied, 'Militant, not triumphant, for you have no power to separate me from the church triumphant to which I go.'

With a final sneer, the hangman checked the noose and gave a mighty heave. Savonarola fell. The noose did its work. He died instantly.

For his persecutors, it was not over. They clamped iron collars around the broken necks of Savonarola and his followers and chained them to the gibbet to hold them longer in the flames. Then the hangman set a torch to the wood and flames quickly engulfed the bodies. Their earthly remains shimmered and blackened in the heat, while boys threw rocks at their flaming bodies for sport. Within an hour, the entire gallows and platform collapsed in flame and smoke; all traces of the bodies had turned to ash. Kneeling before the inferno, surviving followers of Savonarola wept and prayed. They were jeered and kicked by the rabble.

Guards were stationed to bar anyone from sifting through the smouldering ash for relics, and the city council ordered men to gather up every scrap of ash with broom and shovel. The three men's remains were then dumped into the Arno River. Rome was determined that there would be no relic of Savonarola coming back to haunt them in the future. 'Best to commit the friar from Ferarra to memory only,' was the word from the pope. Nevertheless, stories abounded in the years that followed, one insisting that Savonarola's heart was found untouched by the flames and was whisked away by some of his followers.

The ashes had not cooled before police began scouring the city for any of Savonarola's writings. Pamphlets, drawings, printed sermons — everything was gathered up and burned. San Marco, where Savonarola had served as prior, was treated like a plague had passed through it. Given a ceremonial cleansing, its doors were locked shut for three months, after which the library was confiscated, the student dormitory was sold, and hymns, prayers or processions implemented by Savonarola were expunged and forbidden. To complete his degradation, pleasure-loving Florentines sang obscene songs about Savonarola and posted insulting pictures of the friar around the city.

Enduring legacy

But that is only part of the story. Not everyone joined in the revelry at the death of Savonarola. Among his surviving followers was a poet who penned these lines in memory of him.

Charity is extinct,
Love of God is no more.
All are lukewarm;
And without living faith.
Alas! the saint is dead!
Alas! O Lord! Alas!
Thou hast taken our prophet
And drawn him to thyself.

Though the wild parties recommenced in Florence, and though Savonarola was not canonized but cut off from the visible Church, many in Tuscany and Ferrara agreed with this anonymous poet and hailed him as a local saint.

Even Machiavelli later revised his opinion of Savonarola. A political official who benefited greatly from the new government Savonarola helped establish, Machiavelli originally took his stand against the friar. Author of *The Prince*, the manual for pragmatic politicians, who famously said that rulers are better off 'feared than loved' by their subjects, later wrote of Savonarola:

The people of Florence were persuaded by Friar Girolamo Savonarola that he spoke with God. I do not wish to make judgement about whether or not this was true, for one should speak with reverence of such a man as that. But I do want to say that a vast number of people believed it, because his life, his doctrine, and the issues he took up sufficed to make them have faith in him.

Political theorists and painters alike benefited from Savonarola's ministry. His preaching profoundly influenced Florentine painter Botticelli and turned him from painting pornography to producing works that honoured the God of the Bible. Michelangelo, arguably the greatest Renaissance artist, frequently attended worship services led by Savonarola and faithfully read his sermons and other writings. The spirit of Savonarola influenced his incomparable painting of the ceiling of the Sistine Chapel, and the *Last Judgment* behind the altar. Another Renaissance artist, Fra Bartolomeo, painted a portrait of the friar and entitled it with the fitting epithet, 'Portrait of Girolamo of Ferrara, prophet sent by God'.

Gospel legacy

After Savonarola's death, as the Catholic Counter Reformation feverishly laboured to destroy his writings, Savonarola's written works flourished in reprint editions around Europe. Try though he did, it seemed that the pope could not obliterate Savonarola's voice. They could burn the man, but his message lived on. It was a message taken up in the next generation by Reformers like Martin Luther who shouldered Savonarola's mantle, refined it still more precisely, and preached the purity of the gospel of free grace in Christ alone. So appreciative was Luther that he republished Savonarola's *Prison Meditations,* and in his preface he hailed Savonarola as the precursor of his doctrine. 'Although some theological mud still adhered to the feet of that holy man,' wrote Luther, '[Savonarola] nevertheless maintained justification by faith alone without works, and he was burned by the Pope. But lo! he lives in blessedness, and Christ canonized him by our means, although the Pope and the Papists might burst with rage.'

But just what was it about Savonarola that was so offensive to the papacy and the medieval Church that they had to be rid of him?

It was no doubt many things, but perhaps it was his fearless exposé on the unbridled corruption rampant in the church in his day that rankled most. About the clerics at all levels of church hierarchy, Savonarola boldly declared what anyone who didn't live in a cave knew manifestly to be true. 'They tickle men's ears with talk of Aristotle and Plato, Virgil and Petrarch, and take no concern in the salvation of souls.'

This was offensive, but that didn't deter Savonarola; men's souls were at stake. And so he would not be silenced, not even when they offered to make him a cardinal. Unrelenting, he persisted in his denouncements.

> Why, instead of expounding so many books, do they not expound the one Book in which is the law and spirit of life! The Gospel, O Christians, ye should ever have with ye; not merely the letter, but the spirit of the Gospel. For if thou lack the spirit of grace, what will it avail thee to carry about the whole book.

Though he did not live long enough to systematically challenge many Roman Catholic doctrinal errors, there is a great deal more of the gospel of grace in Savonarola than many expect to find. He understood that if we have the whole Bible preached to us but do not have the gospel and the spirit of grace 'ever with us', preaching was without its power and would accomplish nothing in the souls of men. On a trajectory away from medieval theological error, he proclaimed the gospel of grace, according to the light he had been given in his time and place, with a great deal more boldness, zeal and power in his preaching than tragically in many pulpits today.

Just as in the hall of heroes in Hebrews 11 we read of sinful individuals, deeply indebted to grace — Samson, Abraham, Sarah, David — so was Savonarola. Flawed, imperfect, influenced by the superstitions and errors of his day — like all of us; nevertheless, Savonarola was called and equipped of God as a forerunner of reformation in the modern world.

Finally, it is the Bible itself that models the attitude we ought to have toward Christian heroes: 'As for the saints in the land, they are the excellent ones, in whom is all my delight' (Psalm 16:3). Savonarola — warts and all — was one of those excellent ones.

Though his effort to erect a theocracy was misguided and failed, and though he misunderstood the role of further revelation through visions and prophecy in post-apostolic Florence, yet did he do all this without selfish motive or as a pretext for gaining power. There are enormous lessons to learn from Savonarola's complete lack of legacy-building ambition. First and last, he cared about the salvation of souls. And he understood at least on a rudimentary level that salvation and the life of faith 'depends entirely on grace', as he wrote when the flaming spectre of his martyrdom loomed ever closer: 'It is certainly a gratuitous gift of God.' Such single-minded concern makes Savonarola one of the excellent ones in whom all Christians will take delight and find inspiration.

Fittingly, Hebrews' hall of heroes concludes by directing our attention away from men and flawed human agents like Savonarola:

> Therefore, since we are surrounded by so great a cloud of witnesses, let us also lay aside every weight, and sin which clings so closely, and let us run with endurance the race that is set before us, looking to Jesus, the founder and perfecter of our faith, who for the joy that was set before him endured the cross, despising the shame, and is seated at the right hand of the throne of God (Hebrews 12:1-2).

Cut through the politics, the prophesying, the confiscation of vanities, the sometimes harsh denouncements, the 'theological mud still adhering to his feet', and it is justice to say that Savonarola knew that outside of the grace of Jesus Christ, '*Siamo perduti!*'; we are, in fact, ruined. Because of this certain knowledge, he attempted to fix all eyes in Florence on 'Jesus, the founder and perfecter of our faith'. For this, Girolamo Savonarola deserves the regard of every Christian, in every age, who loves and delights in the gospel of Jesus Christ.

Further reading

William and Ariel Durant, *The Renaissance.*

Rachel Erlanger, *The Unarmed Prophet, Savonarola in Florence.*

Lauro Martinez, *Fire in the City, Savonarola and the Struggle for the Soul of Renaissance Florence.*

Ralph Roeder, *The Man of the Renaissance.*

Philip Schaff, *History of the Christian Church.*

Paschale Villari, *Life of Savonarola.*